Reputation Shift

5 High Performance Truths for Success:
Lessons from Pit Road to the Boardroom

It takes 20 years to build a good reputation and five minutes to ruin it.
If you think about that, you'll do things differently.

—Warren Buffett

D1241866

What Others Are Saying . . .

"The book of Proverbs says that a good name is better than silver. But I know from experience that you have to work hard and be diligent to keep it once you have it. And, if you get selfish or careless, you will pay a price, especially these days. If you want to build a great reputation, Mike Mooney has put all the tools you'll need in one place. *Reputation Shift* is wise, and it's practical. I highly recommend it."

—*Darrell Waltrip, NASCAR Hall of Fame Driver and FOX Sports Analyst*

"If you are building your personal brand—and you should be—Mike Mooney can help. *Reputation Shift* is a timely and practical textbook for succeeding in the always connected, always on world. Real, practical advice, delivered in a contemporary and highly readable package."

—*Seth Farbman, Chief Marketing Officer, Spotify*

"Mike Mooney understands a vital success principle: It takes a lifetime to build a reputation and only a minute to lose it. *Reputation Shift*, with its five powerful rules, should be the handbook for anyone who understands the true value of how others see us."

—*First Sergeant Matt Eversmann, US Army (retired) member of Task Force Ranger whose actions were depicted in the movie Black Hawk Down*

REPUTATION *SHIFT*

5 High Performance Truths For Success

REPUTATION SHIFT

Lessons from Pit Road to the Boardroom

MIKE MOONEY

Entrepreneur Press
7300 W. Joy Road
Dexter, MI 48130

Published 2018 by Entrepreneur Press

Printed in the United States of America
Design by Thomson Shore, Inc.

ISBN: 978-1-943290-46-8
Library of Congress Control Number: 2018932022

ROAD MAP

FOREWORD

The subject of one's reputation is an important one, and one that is certainly not spoken of or taught enough today. Enter Mike Mooney and this important effort he has undertaken in examining the subject. In introducing this book for Mike, which is a great honor, I want to underscore three key points about what Mike writes about and what you will find within these pages—timelessness, favor, and wisdom.

TIMELESSNESS

The first place my mind goes on the subject of reputation is back thousands of years to King Solomon and Proverbs 22:1: "A good name is more desirable than great riches; to be esteemed is better than silver or gold."

These words ring as true today as they did in the time of King Solomon. As the centuries have passed, things like quality of life and technological advances have all changed and evolved, but the importance of one's reputation remains as critical as ever.

As CEO of a leading executive search firm in sports, I can tell you we deal with this subject daily. One of the first questions our clients will want to know about a candidate is what their reputation is like, and one of the major parts of our job is finding that out for them.

The enduring importance of one's reputation is simply a subject that King Solomon was right about, your parents were right about, I am right about, and as you'll soon see, Mike Mooney is exactly right about.

FAVOR

Let me tell you a quick story.

An acquaintance I knew in Dallas was out of a job. He had been in real estate, been a college basketball coach, and done some other things. He had always wanted to become an athletic director but never acted on that dream. Because of God's good timing, an athletic director position opened at a small college near his hometown. I spent some time with him and prepared him for the interview, but we both knew the odds could be long because there would be many candidates with much better professional preparation for the job.

The odds evened out considerably once he got to the interview. He quickly discovered that the chair of the search committee at the school knew his dad, who had recently passed away. Not only did the chair know his dad, but he had great stories about how kind and helpful his dad had been to him early in his career. Needless to say, the interview sailed from there and our guy got the job.

What is amazing was the differentiating factor here was the generational blessing his dad passed on to him through reputation. You and I build our reputation every day. But the benefits and blessings of our reputation may not always be realized by us, instead they could be paid forward to our children and our grandchildren. In the case of our guy who became the athletic director, his greatest strength was the reputation his father had built fifty years earlier!

WISDOM

Mike Mooney's seven chapters are so full of wisdom that I cannot neatly summarize it for you here. In fact, even if I could—I wouldn't! You have to read the book, it is too valuable!

However, I do want to preview a few particularly wise areas of the book for you to look forward to. In chapter 2, he asks if you are withdrawing more in life than you are depositing. I always say the difference between successful people and unsuccessful people are good questions, and really good questions sometimes call for uncomfortable introspection. That is what Mike does here. In chapter 3, Mike introduces the "Reputation Equation." Now I love when someone is smart enough to actually create a formula, and what Mike does is show how reputation is equal to "Values + Decisions + Behavior + Time." And then in chapter 7, Mike lays out the four steps for repairing a damaged reputation. That could be a book or a college course just itself. This chapter offers hope for those reading this book who may need to repair their reputation. You're never too late!

I suggest you read this book several times because the insights offered are gold to those who follow these great nuggets of wisdom.

—Bob Beaudine,
Author of the bestselling book *The Power of WHO!* and *2 Chairs*

ACKNOWLEDGMENTS

I WOULD LIKE TO EXPRESS my sincere gratitude to the many people who supported me through the years-long process of writing this book! Anyone who has attempted something outside of their comfort zone knows the power and value of friendship during the moments of question and doubt.

Without the love, patience, and belief of my wife, Krista, children, Alexa, Blair, and Brooke, and my parents, I'm not sure I would have been able to "birth" this book! I'd specifically like to thank the following people who guided me, supported me, and kept me moving forward:

Mark Ethridge, Bob Beaudine, Darrell Waltrip, Seth Farbman, Chad Solomonson, Jason Solomonson, Daryl Solomonson, Tom Cotter, Erik Arneson, Maggie Harris, Dennis Welch, Lee Allentuck, Bruce Mosley, Sean Stowers, Jared Nichols, Jim Haigh, Rick Oppedisano, David Jessey, Andy Williamson, Jonathan Catherman, Matt Eversmann, Tori Eversmann, Rodrick Cox, Doug Cox, Trey Siner, Shane Yount, Doug Poppen, Lindsey Alexander, Wally McCarty and Adam Elsedoudi.

INTRODUCTION

IF I WERE TO ASK YOU RIGHT NOW how much your reputation is worth, what would that monetary value be? It's hard to put a value on something that we may think is intangible, right? However, if your personal or brand's reputation were ruined there probably isn't an amount of money you wouldn't pay to get it back. That's the thing about reputations. We typically don't pay much attention to them until they come under fire or the damage has been done.

Think about names such as Lance Armstrong, Bill Cosby, Jared Fogle, and Eliot Spitzer. What images and thoughts come to mind? These are all people who had built up strong credibility and immense respect over many years, but lapses judgment and their subsequent behavior cost them one of their most valuable assets—their reputation.

Reputation management is a passion of mine. For more than two decades, I have worked in the sports industry, the majority of those years in motorsports, and I have seen the positive and negative impact of how reputations influence fan perspective and loyalty toward sponsors, leagues, and athletes. My vantage point has changed over the years. I have worked at sports and entertainment agencies where I crafted scores of account strategies and developed plans to protect and shape brand reputations and served as counsel to executive leaders. There were also several years where I was the corporate sponsor and directed the sports-marketing communications to connect with both internal business units as well as consumers to drive our business forward.

In an effort to bridge my agency and brand experience, I took on a senior executive role for a professional sports organization, where I could truly bring my experiences to bear. My position affords me regular access to CEOs, CMOs, and COOs as well as daily interaction with their agency partners to create award-winning motorsports programs, which is very satisfying. Working in the post–Great Recession sponsorship world certainly presents challenges, but also significant opportunities. One of the biggest opportunities is to evolve the way we do business. When sponsorship dollars were easy to come by, the focus of most organizations was on the transaction—make the deal and get onto the next one. Now, with more competition for sponsorship dollars, the mindset must shift away from the transaction and toward the relationships—the emphasis becomes the lifetime value of a partner and growing business with them. Part of that evolution is the recognition that our reputation is a vital component to business success.

My years in this fast-paced sports industry have given me the rare privilege of working with and representing iconic brands, such as Mercedes-Benz, Walmart, 3M, Sprint, Tylenol, Kellogg's, Lowe's Home Improvement Warehouse, and Sunoco, to name a few. Beyond working directly with motorsports leagues, including NASCAR (National Association of Stock Car Auto Racing), IndyCar, and NHRA (National Hot Rod Association), I have counseled dozens of Fortune 500 leaders and professional athletes on crisis management issues as well as strategies to proactively manage and protect their reputations.

There is no substitute for personal experience when it comes to reputation management, and I've learned a considerable amount through my firsthand experiences ranging from dealing with driver deaths to launching sponsorships worth three-quarters of a billion dollars. I've been witness to athletes shooting off their mouths, costing them millions of dollars in lost endorsement revenue, and I've created communications strategies to change public opinion on controversial issues.

These experiences taught me, over time, numerous lessons. One lesson was about the value and importance of proactively managing, building, and protecting our reputations, regardless of whether those were for brands or for individuals. Another was that, more often than not, when a reputation comes under attack, it's usually because of something that someone did or did not do in the first place—a missed opportunity or a lapse in judgment.

The birth of personal brand development via consumer-generated content and social media has radically shifted the power of conversation and influence over how our personal brand reputations should be managed.

And while reputation management has become a much more prevalent topic over the past decade, through research, I have found numerous references to the high value placed upon our reputations going back several centuries. Yes, even before social media, ancient Roman authors were talking and writing about the powerful influence of reputations with value far outweighing that of money when lost. Publilius Syrus, a first-century Roman author, once wrote a long time ago, "A good reputation is more valuable than money."

Because of technology, we now live in a Reputation Economy where information about us can be learned or shared by just a mouse click. This world allows anyone with access to the Internet a digital voice that can either build or begin to tear down our reputations as well as the ability to hide behind anonymous screen names or handles.

The landscape and rules for personal reputation management have changed forever.

That is why it's time for a reputation shift. The intent of this book is to illustrate how our reputations are not intangible "things." Rather, our reputations are living and evolving assets that can either propel us to new personal or professional heights, or if ignored or mismanaged, can keep us tethered to the ground. The choice, as are most opportunities in life, is yours.

I will both share personal experiences that tested reputations as well as outline mainstream reputation crisis examples to shift your perspective on how you see and value your own reputation. More importantly, you will learn five essential and actionable truths that I know will give you the tools to fully develop and protect your reputation on a daily basis. Regardless of if you are an individual looking to truly transform your reputation or if you are working for a company and responsible for that brand's reputation, these truths will apply for both personal and corporate initiatives.

This book is written with the intent of it being an interactive, reflective, and action-oriented experience—not just a passive reading event. It does not matter if you are a seasoned executive, an emerging leader, an entrepreneur, or a student about to graduate from college, this book and the end-of-chapter exercises will help you fully understand the impact of how your values ground your decision-making process, which leads to actions. Those actions, in turn, become the basis of your reputation.

I once read that when opportunity knocks, it's too late for preparation. You may be looking for your next career opportunity or perhaps trying to take your business to the next level or maybe even trying to attract the right talent to your firm. Better yet, wouldn't it be great if that career opportunity found you? Did you know that more than 85 percent of open jobs are filled by people networking and recommending an individual? Looking for a way to double your business revenue? Considering that 65 percent of new business comes from referrals, it is possible. Wouldn't it be great if top talent sought out your firm? That could happen, because 84 percent of people would leave their current jobs to join a company with a great reputation.

While this book will give you the road map to strengthen and protect your reputation, it will be your effort and commitment that will start to drive the lifelong, transformational change you seek.

It's time for a shift in terms of how we proactively build, manage, and harness the power of our personal reputations. It's time for a reputation shift.

Chapter One

LIVING IN THE REPUTATION ECONOMY

Google is a reputation management system, not a search engine.
—Clive Thompson, Author & Journalist

I POKED MY HEAD INTO MY TEN-YEAR-OLD DAUGHTER'S BED-ROOM after work one day and saw her sitting on her floor surrounded by thousands of small colorful rubber bands—it looked as though she had just robbed an orthodontist's office. These neatly organized piles were actually part of a crafting kit called Rainbow Loom. If you aren't familiar with this rubber bracelet craze, this is a kit of looming tools where kids can weave together small multicolored rubber bands and create individualized bracelets that could represent your favorite country, sports team, college, little league team, charitable cause, military branch—essentially, anything that has a color associated with it can be represented by dozens of small rubber bands woven together and put on your wrist for all to see.

When my daughter first got this kit, we would inevitably vacuum up more rubber bands from the carpet than what actually made it into the bracelet. But, she worked at mastering the various braids. Yes, there is the "fishtail" (and don't forget the "triple fishtail" as well as the "inverted fishtail"), "tidal wave," "rock candy," "arrow stitch," "double cross," "warrior," "the cube," "double starburst," "firecracker," "triple link chain"—honestly, many of them looked like just twisted mistakes that someone just gave a name to because they spent so much time making it. Nonetheless, she watched countless "how to" videos on YouTube of kids teaching other kids how to effortlessly loom and crank out enough of these to make even the toughest manufacturing floor manager proud. She got very good at making these bracelets and began selling them to her friends at school and in the neighborhood. And, yes, as a supportive dad, I did wear (and pay for) several of them—oddly enough, they actually became a conversation starter at business events when one dad would see them and ask the question, "So, how old is your kid?"

I could see her working intently on her bed with a plastic loom on her lap, what looked like one of those clear plastic fishing tackle organizers full of colored rubber bands next to her, and a long sheet of paper on her nightstand. So, I walked into her room and said, "Hey, you. How was your day?"

"It was a very good day at school!" she said.

"That's great to hear, sweetheart. Did you learn something new in class or go on a field trip?" I asked.

"Nope. I got five more orders for bracelets. See my order sheet?" I looked at her order sheet and sure enough there were five more names next to the fifteen other names ahead of them.

I won't lie, there was a big sense of pride welling up inside me at this point. And I was excited that she was experiencing some success in her first entrepreneurial endeavor. I thought that would be a great experience for her—setting goals, making mistakes and learning from them, recognizing the value of her time, customer service, inventory management, etc. But, then she said something that just put me back on my heels, something that I did not expect her to understand the value of at such an early age.

"Dad, I'm really excited about getting all of these orders," she said. "I've got a really good reputation with the kids in my classes for my bracelets. They're telling other kids and it's really helping my business."

And there it is. That is the heart of the message I want to share with you in this book—and it came from a fourth grader. Those three sentences, while simple in a little girl's world, frame up the power of our reputations and the impact that a reputation can have on your business, your brand, your career, and your life—whether you're selling rubber band bracelets, consulting services, or a consumer product.

The rise and prominence of social media has solidified the phenomenon of personal branding. Simply, this allows individuals to take their passions, skills, and experience or interests in a particular field and cast a far-reaching social net in an effort to connect with other like-minded people or groups, develop a social following, and increase their influence, which creates personal and professional fulfillment and opportunities.

Social media has not only changed the landscape of how we connect, share, interact, and relate to one another, it's also driven up the value of something that many had once considered an intangible asset. Something that if I asked you to put a price on, you'd be hard-pressed to come up with a dollar figure for its value, but if you lost it, you'd probably pay anything to get it back—your reputation.

The Reputation Economy

Have you heard of Jamie Oliver? His story is a unique one, but it further demonstrates the power of what can be accomplished when passions, action, word of mouth, and social media intersect.

Jamie grew up in a family that ran a well-known pub in Clavering, England. His culinary reputation grew throughout Europe during the 2000s as he apprenticed with some of the best culinary talent while also making appearances on television shows, writing books, and developing theater performances where he talked about the power of food—not just how it sustains us, but about the ease of food preparation, the need to make healthy choices, and that there had to be a focus on childhood food education.

His message and purpose took root in a variety of highly impactful educational programs and life-changing school initiatives in Europe. Jamie took his activism to another level in 2010 when he launched the United States-focused *Food Revolution*. Unfortunately, the United States leads the global community in food-related health issues, so he took his message and began a mission of education across the country. Beyond the usual means of event promotion—television news and specials as well as radio and print interviews—Jamie continued to leverage the power of social media and the global scale of these channels to build advocates, deliver key messages, and increase his influence. As a result, his followers on Twitter and Facebook channels have each eclipsed six million followers, and he has another five million-plus people checking him out on Instagram.

The ease and impact of connecting with that many people globally would not be possible without social media channels. Such a powerful platform allows Jamie to educate, inspire, create change, and, ultimately, build his brand by making a positive difference in the world and allowing people the opportunity to join him on his journey and participate in his mission.

Reputations are earned over years of consistent actions and behaviors, but in today's world of instantaneous information gathering and citizen journalists tweeting and posting, reputations can be galvanized or shattered in moments.

Social media has ushered in a new type of economy. This economy is rooted in your track record of actions, decisions, and behavior and how that has been shared, judged, or perceived.

While those assessments might be subjective or considered unfair, the reality is that doesn't matter because we now live in the court of public opinion and operate in a Reputation Economy.

In an August 27, 2010, article on Forbes.com titled "Making Money in the Reputation Economy," writer Anthony Johndrow, partner and managing director of the Reputation Institute, deftly described the economy in which we now live. Johndrow wrote, "Like the 'innovation economy' of the 1990s or the 'risk decade' of the 2000s, the 2010s promise to be where reputation is activated as a driving force behind markets." Social connectivity is now the traffic signal at the intersection of your brand and your reputation.

The Oracle of Omaha, Warren Buffett, said it best, "If you lose dollars for the firm by bad decisions, I will be understanding. If you lose reputation for the firm, I will be ruthless."

Guess what? You are the firm. You are the CEO of your life. You should be ruthless with how you manage your reputation because of the power it has to transform your life and business. And whether that is a positive transformation or a negative one is completely up to you!

Large corporations face the same challenges as we do. Traditionally, companies would define and leverage competitive differentiators such as depth of product lines, highly trained people, market penetration, or sheer organizational scale. As margins get slimmer, as customer choices increase, and as marketers clamber to bring to market the next "it" product, more brands are recognizing the power and impact of reputations.

Welcome to the Court of Public Opinion

Social engagement between corporations and customers has created a new dynamic. This dynamic is based upon in relationships where customers aren't just data points in spreadsheets—they are individuals with global and influential voices. And what they say or post online about a company, its people, products, or services can build a brand as quickly as it can damage or even destroy one. Consider that 92 percent of consumers trust peer recommendations, while only 14 percent trust advertising. Why is that? For the same reason that four out of five consumers changed their minds about a purchase solely on negative information they found online. Simply put, we now have global outlets to share our experiences and interactions and search engines that help organize them for easy and nearly instantaneous access—and we often trust each other (even if there is no preexisting relationship) more than we trust a corporation.

This drives home the new reality that a reputation cannot be provided by a "Made in the USA" label or offshored to reduce production costs. For corporate brands, reputations are crafted and managed (or mismanaged) every day from the highest executive suites to the cubicles where employees earn hourly wages. This is no different for individuals, who can have their popularity skyrocket or fall from grace based on their behaviors.

What comes to mind when you hear the names Enron, Goldman Sachs, Harvey Weinstein, Tiger Woods, Anthony Weiner, and Lance Armstrong? Those are corporations or individuals whose reputations were damaged by their own behavior and decisions, and whether right or wrong, were found guilty in the court of public opinion. Besides the personal embarrassment, there were significant financial losses and negative impacts to their future corporate/personal earning potential as well as careers.

All of these people and companies lost reputational equity, career opportunities, and money and tarnished their legacies. But the reality is that for each of them, there was a moment of choice. There was a moment when a slight pause—a few seconds of reflection to think "what if?"—could have changed the outcome of what they experienced.

However, social channels come with a double-edged proposition. With their ability to instantaneously share information globally to humor us, educate us, or inspire us, they also carry the power to tear people down, just as quickly as the information is downloaded onto the latest digital device. Why is this? It's because not only is news shared, but people are also sharing their experiences. That is how reputations are often developed, either through firsthand experience or by hearing about others' experiences.

KNOWLEDGE IS POWER AND POWER HAS INFLUENCE

Regardless of the positive or negative status of a reputation, the bottom line is that reputations are just as valuable to an individual or organization as the products and services they market. Reputations are a vital link between brands and customers in a period where options and information are a mere search term away. Reputations are the foundation and relational touchpoints for boutique shops fighting for their share in aggressive markets. Reputations are a key competitive differentiator.

The Forbes.com article also cited Morten Albaek, the chief marketing officer of Vestas, a Danish wind energy corporation, as saying, "Today, we serve two and only two masters: revenue and reputation. The trick is to position your brand and build your reputation in the sweet spot between capitalism and humanism."

Let's look at the idea that fusing reputations and business is not just a novel concept for today's Reputation Economy, rather, it's a key link in the customer relationship chain.

Customer expectations about how a brand will engage with them, help them, and understand them are at levels never seen before. Why is this? One of the most significant drivers of those expectations is knowledge. We've all heard that knowledge is power, and in the digital world in which we live, knowledge is in our hands, our purses, or back pockets in the form of smartphones.

This has radically shifted the balance of power between consumers and brands.

Most, if not all, consumer brands have a shopper marketing division. These are the people who study the "whys" of shopper behavior and decisions. They work to understand, unravel, and create consumer "shopping occasions" to change how brands position themselves in the retail environment in an effort to meet the needs of various customer segments during specific times of the year and ultimately sell more product.

Proctor & Gamble first used the phrase "first moment of truth" (FMOT) in 2005 to identify the moment after consumers have been made aware of a product by advertising or word of mouth—essentially, the moment when consumers would decide whether to purchase a product or not. P&G contended that the FMOT was when the shopper saw the product on the shelf. While the FMOT was an important time stamp for marketers to understand how their product went from shelf to shopping cart, there was also a second moment of truth (SMOT), which was also an important element in the consumer purchasing cycle. The SMOT was identified as the moment of use, or experience, when the consumer's need was satisfied by the product, thus creating brand or product loyalty.

That all changed when Google unleashed its e-book *Winning the Zero Moment of Truth* in 2011. The theory of ZMOT built upon the existing P&G model but shed light on the pre-FMOT purchasing process that consumers now employ given their access to information.

Jim Lecinski, the author of *Winning the Zero Moment of Truth*, asserted that consumers are still made aware of the products through advertising and word of mouth channels, but before they even step foot inside a brick and mortar store, they are scouring the Internet for product information and user reviews. The period of time when the consumer is searching and reading about the product to gain insight and knowledge to shape his or her purchasing decision is the ZMOT.

According to a 2011 Google study, 88 percent of US consumers engage in ZMOT behavior before making their final purchase decisions. In fact, consumers sought out product information, on average, through 10.4 digital or traditional sources before making a purchase decision. The Google study goes on to say that that is twice the number of channels sought out in 2010; it grew to 12 sources in 2012 and continues to grow today. We do this almost instinctively now when considering buying everything from paint to cars. We tend to look at the manufacturer information for what the product will do as well as its promise and benefits, but what often carries more weight are the user reviews, which gives us validation from our peers. Those reviews were written by consumers whose experiences shaped the reputations of products and brands.

Driving Your Success in the Reputation Economy

It's clear to see that because of social media channels, succeeding in the Reputation Economy is not only a challenge that corporate brands face, but something that individual people can win at, too.

Just as corporations need to evolve in how they meet their business goals, so must we, as individuals, entrepreneurs, or entertainers, as we work toward our own success. Only you can define what success looks like. Is it a promotion from your current position? Is it starting your own agency? Is it the ability to attract top talent to your company and keep it? Perhaps it's finding a new job or, better yet, that new opportunity finding you based upon your reputation for what you do.

Remember how easily consumers leverage accessible information about a brand's products or services before investing the time to walk into a store or make an online purchase? Well, executive recruiters, human resources managers, talent scouts as well as top-level brass will have their ZMOT when they access information about recruits before even picking up the phone or sending an email to a potential candidate.

Search-engine technology can provide unbelievably focused streams of information at the touch of a "return" or "go" key. At the same time, it has also created a Wild West environment where the rules of engagement are being written and rewritten while people are pioneering new ways of getting things done.

Whether it's people who are underemployed seeking out the slightest competitive edge or someone looking to start their own business—a reputation has become a crucial and legitimate differentiator.

Your reputation is your competitive edge as you drive toward success. It cannot be overlooked in a market where what people say about you or your company can have either a positive or negative monetary impact.

In 2011, Booz Allen Hamilton, a global management consulting firm, did a study on the financial impact on organizations who suffered self-inflicted reputation setbacks. The study helped link the impact of reputation issues to companies' bottom lines. It found that shareholder value, on average, dropped 33 percent within one year of a negative situation becoming public news. Reputation setbacks can have similarly harmful impacts on individuals.

"HEY, I'M LOOKING FOR SOMEONE WHO CAN . . ."

Let's look at the power of your most natural resource in another light. Think of a time when a colleague, friend, or recruiter asked you if a person you knew would be a good fit for a position. What did you say? What did you reflect upon to give your answer? Whether you know it or not, you tapped into two "information banks" that we all use to give someone a recommendation or hire someone to do a job for you.

The first area that you sift through is your own personal experience. You think back to your firsthand interactions, which include how the person represented himself, the language they used, the way they explained how they approached and solved a problem—did they actually do what they said they would?

11

Did they do it with good style? These are just some of the mental Google searches you quickly make when assessing a reputation.

If you don't have the first-person experience, then you typically access the second area of insight—what you've heard about that person from others whom you trust. It's their experience *and* your relationship with that person that allows you to accept a perception that hasn't been shaped by your own interaction.

That's the power, influence, value, and, at times, subjective nature of reputations. The responsibility of developing, managing, and nurturing your reputation is on your shoulders, however, others have a say in what your reputation is, too. For that reason alone, you must be vigilant and diligent in how you harness the power of and shift your perspective on personal reputation management.

I mentioned earlier that just as consumers can access insight, experiences, and information about products and services, so do recruiters. The reality is that we all have ZMOT channels in our lives—they are our social networks.

It's common sense that your posts, pictures, feedback, and other online contributions as well as the posts, pictures, and comments that others make that include you, are all available for public review 24/7/365. I'm sure you can think of several headlines about times when someone lost a job or was reprimanded because of something they posted or something that was posted about them. How about employees who thought that pranks on customers would be seen as humorous, only to find themselves out of work and with a company in an all-hands-on-deck crisis situation fighting a social media backlash? Like I said, it should be common sense, right? But, then again, as Will Rogers once said, "Common sense ain't common."

Working to get ahead is not an uncommon mission—never has been and never will be. There are people who are always focused on moving forward with their careers, developing new skills, or expanding other life pursuits. While specialized training, education, on-the-job experience, performance, relationships, and reputation have all played key roles in that progress—and, again, always will—the difference today is the immediate impact of and access to information about individuals. When we drill down into what is being shared, it is often rooted in behavior. Why is behavior so important? I know that seems like a ridiculous question (and it even felt that way when I wrote this!), but can you think of a story you've heard about a coworker's behavior that resulted in them getting passed over for the promotion or additional responsibility they wanted? Can you recall a story in the news about a person's behavior that caused them to get reprimanded or fired?

Prior to the Internet, those stories were limited to word of mouth or local news. You might hear about it at the water cooler or local coffee shop and that was the extent of the conversation. Today's word of mouth is spread at 140-plus characters or more on other social media channels, and the Internet never forgets. So, not only does the story spread on a global level, it becomes part of their reputation halo, which we'll dig into later in the book, and stays with the person for years to come.

Take for example George Ciccariello-Maher who is an assistant professor of history and politics at Drexel University in Pennsylvania. On Christmas Eve, the assistant professor tweeted, "All I Want for Christmas is White Genocide."

Ironically, Ciccariello-Maher is white. He felt it necessary to follow up his tweet by posting, "To clarify: when the whites were massacred during the Haitian revolution, that was a good thing indeed."

The university became aware of the tweet and issued a statement that said the comments were "utterly reprehensible, deeply disturbing, and do not in any way reflect the values of the University." However, Drexel released another statement that went on to shine a vital light on the importance of thinking about what we post because of social media's significant impact, yet limited ability to convey context.

Drexel's statement read, in part, "The wide range of reactions to his tweets suggests that his intentions were not adequately conveyed. These responses underscore the importance of choosing one's words thoughtfully and exercising appropriate judgment in light of the inherent limitations presented by communications on social media."

Have you heard about the freshman at Belmont University in Tennessee who decided to make a racist post on Snapchat? Justin Woodard was apparently fed up with athletes protesting the American flag during the national anthem and took a picture of a television screen showing several Philadelphia Eagles players raising their fists in a symbol of black power. He then decided to post a racism-laced rant that included his thought that the athletes needed a "damn bullet in their head," and ended with, "if you don't like this country, then get the hell out." Someone who saw the Snapchat took a screenshot and then posted it, which caused it to go viral.

The Belmont University administration immediately got involved, issuing a statement that the comments did not align with the institution's values. Within twenty-four hours, Woodard was no longer a student at Belmont.

Do you think he'll have any problems getting into another college when the admissions team does a preliminary Internet search? How about if he finds getting into another college is just too much and he decides to just get a job? Do you think the HR department or hiring manager will have second thoughts about hiring him when they come across the news stories?

I am not supporting or excusing the behavior above, but I do believe people have the right to their own opinions. The examples above are extreme. However, they boil down to thinking through decisions and the behavior they lead to—is acting in a certain manner the right thing to do? Is it in the right forum? Will it spark positive dialogue and exchanges? What is the context, and will it be lost via social media channels?

Bottom line is that short-term behavior can have long-term implications if left unchecked—both positive and negative!

Consider that to get a great job, you need a competitive edge. It's essential, and your reputation can help it or harm it. Want to see the power of reputations on employment? Do a quick Google search and you'll be presented with tens of thousands of links about how to use your reputation to land your next job, how to sabotage your own future via social media missteps, or how to "bury" the bad information out there on the World Wide Web to better position your reputation.

One Degree of Behavior

The compass is one of the greatest inventions that mankind has created, in my opinion. For centuries, this tool was the lifeblood of explorers, trailblazers, and visionaries who set off to find new adventures, trade routes, territories, and people.

The compass can also be a virtual grounding point for us all in today's social media-fueled society.

To me, that is where the power of the compass comes to life.

Imagine you are heading out on a journey. You've charted your course on your map and have your compass in hand, but there is one problem. You realize that you are one degree off of the proper heading. Now, one degree doesn't sound like a big deal, right? That's just a little off course. It's not like you are heading in the completely wrong direction.

Being off one degree over a short period of time won't completely ruin your trip. Realistically, if you were to walk for one mile at one degree off your plotted course, you will be ninety-two feet away from your intended location. At ninety-two feet, you can still see where you should have been and easily reset your map for the rest of your trip. That scenario from a short-term perspective has an easy solution.

What if you didn't realize after the first mile of your journey that you were one degree off on your compass bearing? Well, being off by only one degree, over time, will lead you way off course and away from your intended destination. For example, if you were flying from Charlotte, North Carolina, to Los Angeles and were one degree off, you would end up nearly fifty miles away from LAX. That's not even in the same zip code!

Reputations are built by consistent behavior over time and not just online, but in our day-to-day interactions with others, in the things we say or don't say, and by the things we do or don't do. The key words in that last sentence are "over time," which means you must approach personal reputation management from a long-term perspective.

More than ever, we must identify what I call the "one degree of behavior" in our daily lives. It's that moment when you think about short-term gains versus the long-term rewards. I have a compass at my desk as a visual reminder that just one degree can change the direction of my journey. The compass can serve as a personal resource and tool in order to navigate the rapids that can leave us personally or professionally either run aground or sailing on to better horizons.

SHIFT POINTS:

- Technology has forever changed how personal brands are created and developed

- Just like customers look for product reviews prior to purchase, so do recruiters prior to making hiring decisions

- Reputations are tangible assets, which when harnessed and managed properly, will make leaders more influential and effective

- Leaders must look to the long-term impact of their decisions and actions instead of short-term gains—one degree of behavior

- Reputations are not only influenced by an individual's actions, but also by what others say or post, regardless of accuracy

- What you do and/or say can easily be recorded and shared, which either hinders or helps your efforts as a leader

ACCELERATION:

1. List five ways you can leverage technology and social media to strengthen your personal brand.

    PERSONAL BRAND DRIVER 1

    _____

    _____

    PERSONAL BRAND DRIVER 2

    _____

    _____

    PERSONAL BRAND DRIVER 3

    _____

    _____

    PERSONAL BRAND DRIVER 4

    _____

    _____

    PERSONAL BRAND DRIVER 5

    _____

    _____

2. What kind of picture would a recruiter or customer piece together by looking at your social media channels, or by talking with your peers, colleagues, or other customers?

    PICTURE PERFECT?

    _____

    _____

    _____

    _____

3. Write down the names of two people in your life whose reputations make them successful. Then write down what their reputations are.

REPUTATION SUCCESS 1

_____

_____

REPUTATION SUCCESS 2

_____

_____

4. On a scale of 1–5 (1 being "hardly ever" and 5 being "all the time"), how often do long-term results factor into your daily decision-making process?

_____

5. Fill in the rest of the sentence . . . I believe my reputation is,

_____

_____

because I consistently

_____

_____

and I believe this to be true because

_____

_____

_____

Chapter Two

Truth Number 1: Open the Bank of You

"Are They Building Grenades or Engines?"

A good reputation is more valuable than money.
—Publilius Syrus, Roman Author

CURRENCY. IT COMES IN MANY FORMS, but whether you are employed or looking for employment, recognize that beyond experience, your reputation is the strongest currency you have.

Imagine that you carry two ATM cards in your wallet. Both give you the ability to deposit or withdraw currency from the bank, however, you own one of the banks—the Bank of You.

I had the opportunity to run the public relations program for Mercedes-Benz's sports platform back in the late '90s, which included IndyCar, ATP World Tour tennis, and PGA TOUR golf, and we found ourselves in a situation where we needed to make some withdrawals! It was the heyday of open-wheel racing and sponsorships, when chefs were flown from Germany to the United States to prepare and present meals for executives at race events.

There were global press junkets, lavish parties, and gifts. It was an amazing time to be in the sport.

Our public relations team worked with five teams and drivers such as Helio Castroneves, who gained additional fame by being the season winner on *Dancing with the Stars*, Al Unser Jr., Patrick Carpentier, and the late Greg Moore, to name a few.

Mercedes-Benz was one of several engine manufacturers in the sport, with a racing heritage that had spanned more than one hundred years, and our German colleagues were focused on nothing less than perfection and winning. Their reentry into the sport in 1994, after nearly a half-century hiatus from IndyCar, was rewarded by Roger Penske's domination at the Indianapolis 500. Since that race, Mercedes-Benz collected checkered flags, trophies, and, in 1997, the coveted Manufacturers' Championship—a title that was last won by Mercedes-Benz in 1955 when Juan Manuel Fangio won the Formula One World Championship. There began a reversal of fortunes in 1998 as many of the Mercedes-Benz teams weren't even seeing the end of the race due to engine failures. In some cases, the engines weren't completing thirty laps before belching smoke and spewing fluids all over the track.

As this became more and more the norm at these races, I recall one journalist who asked me, "Are they building grenades or engines?"

The regular nature of these malfunctions made our postrace reports, which were sent to media outlets, sponsors, and partners, nearly unbearable to write—creative, but still unbearable. I mean how many ways can you write that an engine expired? Sometimes we'd joke about just changing the name of the track and date of the race and leave in the previous week's report. The team engineers and engine builders were frantically trying to figure out what was going on with their power plants, and my PR team worked just as hard to save face (both ours and our client's) among the media corps, since Mercedes-Benz had such a strong competitive run over the previous years.

And this is where solid relationships saved us. You are only as good as your relationships in the PR world—and that is no different with our relationships in this Reputation Economy in which we live. After years of planting relational seeds—essentially developing, nurturing, and making reputation "deposits," it was time to withdraw some "funds" from our Reputation Bank—back to the earlier analogy, the Bank of You.

We huddled with our key journalist contacts and explained that Mercedes was working on the fix to counteract the current dramatic turn in performance. This was an important step and use of energy as the reporters needed this information in order to do their jobs. We couldn't ask them to not write stories—that would not only be insulting, but would probably instigate deeper probes into the situation. We also knew that if we just kept silent, the reporters would have still written their stories about Mercedes's competitive fall from grace. Instead, we ensured that our message points were being delivered and used. Remember that without information, media members, *just like friends, colleagues, or competitors*, are left to speculate, and speculation is the breeding ground for rumors. Silence is never a good strategy when you are managing your reputation.

From a public relations perspective, we couldn't control the engines, their reliability, and on-track performance, but we could control our message and the way we crafted stories for our client. My team began developing media stories and programs that emphasized things that were working, such as Mercedes's production cars, and tied those to PGA TOUR and ATP Tour and lifestyle events while still using our IndyCar drivers in those efforts. We shifted focus away from what was happening on track to what was cool off the track, while maintaining a racing connection. For example, we created the Mercedes-Benz Serves and Curves event that brought together our IndyCar drivers and ATP Tour tennis players with lifestyle and sports media for a day of interactive skills demonstrations. One aspect of the event was the temporary road course we built in a parking lot, where we had our drivers take the journalists around the course in high-performance Mercedes-Benz consumer cars and then let the journalists take their turn with the driver sitting in the passenger seat coaching them. Over time, with consistent effort, creative execution, and tapping into established relationships, it worked.

While proactively pushing new storylines and monitoring the engine developments, we continued to leverage our media relationships to reduce the number of negative stories. While the post-race finishing orders reflected the less-than-desired performance, there were few feature stories shining a critical spotlight on us.

Seeing Blind Spots

OK, so how can you use this in your life to manage your reputation, your brand?

Think for a moment of someone you know who is either employed or between jobs, someone whose reputation will hold them back from either getting a promotion or getting an offer letter, and they just can't understand why, interview after interview, they don't get hired or get the opportunity to work on the next big project.

This person is not necessarily a bad person. They may be someone who has not deliberately managed their reputation or thought about the impact of their decisions and behavior. Maybe they are constantly late for work. Perhaps they are consistently ten minutes late for meetings, sending a message that they don't value other people's time. It could be that little details are not priorities, and the quality of their work might be lower than what is expected at their level, which makes collaboration a painful experience.

This person may be extremely knowledgeable in their field or have a huge heart and is the first to support a charitable cause—again, not a bad person at heart—but a person's behaviors, consistently over time, are the building blocks of a reputation.

In some cases, the behavior is a case of lacking maturity and experience. Or maybe someone hasn't taken them aside and made them aware of the work expectations or their personal blind spots. The reality is that we all have blind spots in our personal and professional lives. Perhaps friends or mentors have spoken with them about the areas where they can improve, and they chose not to do anything with that feedback.

Have you ever had to a similar experience? Have you had the "blind spot" conversation? Maybe you were on the receiving side of the conversation? Regardless of if you are delivering or receiving the message, it takes courage to be in that situation and stay open to what is being said. It is a gift if someone is taking the time to have this conversation with you in a productive manner. I know it may not seem like that if you are hearing the feedback, but these are delicate situations with an underlying message of "you are valued." While our human DNA has us wired to avoid uncomfortable and painful situations, and these types of conversations can be easily put into the uncomfortable category, try to keep an open mind to what is being said. If you trust the person who is delivering the message, then trust the message.

Take a Look at Your Bank Statement

Your Reputation Bank account balance is either increasing or decreasing every day and is based on every action and decision, better yet transaction, that you make—right or wrong. Like many companies today, the Bank of You is open 24/7/365, and more importantly, your balance can be a matter of public opinion and discussion.

Remember, your reputation speaks for you when you are not there to speak for yourself. It is more memorable than your website or business card and, in our saturated social-media world, is always subject to review without your knowledge.

Do a quick online search for "online reputation management" (ORM) or "search engine optimization" (SEO) and you'll find dozens of companies that provide online "scrubbing" services to both individuals and companies that are concerned with negative posts or reviews that have been posted by disgruntled employees, consumers, and in some cases, the competition.

Current statistics show that less than 10 percent of people will go past the first page of web search results. So, ORM and SEO can provide a needed service in the reputation management business by highlighting the good and burying or pushing bad posts deeper in the search pages where, based on what we know about human behavior, they won't be seen.

While the internet allows instantaneous access to information, let's be clear that the core element of personal reputation management truly is our *analog,* day-to-day, face-to-face behavior, which becomes the foundation of anyone's reputation.

Setting Up Your Account

Here are four components to consider when evaluating the Bank of You and what is in your reputation account:

1. Relationships count and are paramount for success. Just like we did with the media, you should establish, nurture, and maintain personal and professional relationships. These are the people who will stand by your side when you are trying to fix your own "engine" issues. Think about it this way: if a good friend of yours said they needed your help to overcome a challenge, I'm sure you would do whatever you could to help, right? So don't be afraid to ask the same of them. Just as humans are wired to avoid pain and discomfort, as I wrote earlier, we are also wired to help and to be empathetic, especially to those we know and care about. Focus on your relationships every day—a personal note, a phone call, or even an email with a link to a story they would appreciate will go a long way. I have a close friend who suspends work each Friday at noon so that the people in his company can spend the rest of the afternoon calling and connecting or reconnecting with friends or old colleagues just to check in and catch up. The principle here is to give and connect without the expectation of getting something immediately back. You give for giving's sake. But, at the same time, you know you are building up your relational currency. It's a brilliant strategy for my friend's business because he has found that over time he generates more business from those Friday calls than he and his team do during any other day of the week. Building relationship management into your reputation management game plan will increase your Bank of You account balance.

2. Diversify—there is strength in building your reputation currency in multiple accounts. Sometimes the first instinct is to run from or ignore a situation when a problem arises. The reality is that the problem will eventually go away. But at what cost? If it's a work situation, people will move on and other issues will arise and the current situation will just be a blip on the radar screen. We see this daily with the minute-by-minute news cycle. You need to recognize, though, that while the situation will blow over and people's attention will shift elsewhere, the impact to you and your reputation can live beyond that moment in time. The choice is yours, and it depends solely on how you handle the situation.

The key is not to withdraw from the various aspects of your life. The basic model of a mutual fund is a great way to show how you can draw from different areas of your life to find a solution. You can work to fix the problem by finding and engaging other areas in your life to focus and draw support—your church community, a local civic group, or professional organization. Stay involved and don't crawl into a shell. Consider volunteering your time and talents to a local college, hospital, or charity. That approach will demonstrate your resolve and resilience, and, if done for the right reasons, you can have a positive impact on others while you work on what might be "broken." The bottom line is that you can build relationships to help you rebuild your reputation!

3. Are you withdrawing more than depositing? Let's face it, we aren't perfect all of the time. None of us are. However, our daily decisions, actions, words, and interactions are either making deposits or withdrawals from the Bank of You. In a world of 140-word Twitter blasts, Facebook posts, highly trafficked customer review sites, and 24/7 media outlets it's more critical than ever to be mindful of how your consistent actions and behavior mold and impact your reputation. A proactive approach to personal reputation management will be one of your greatest resources when building the Bank of You. An honest, introspective look at ourselves easily allows us to recognize how we treat and respect others on a daily basis. An honest conversation with colleagues, friends, and family will immediately let you know if you are taking too much out too often. A conversation like this could start as simple as, "Hey, I've been spending some time thinking about my relationships and I want to make sure that I'm giving as much as I'm getting from friends like you. Do you feel that is the case with our relationship? Where could I help you more? Where can I be a better friend?" People are more willing to give you a mulligan or two when your reputation account is strong as opposed to when you continually overdraft. As with any bank account, there are overdraft fees and penalties!

4. Do you have an interest-bearing account? Don't you love it when your money makes money? At the Bank of You, your account can grow on a daily basis when you have a strong reputation. I can't get away from the thought that your reputation truly speaks for you when you aren't there to speak for yourself, and that's exactly the principle behind having an interest-bearing personal reputation account. Consider these questions as an indicator of the interest you are or aren't earning: are people recommending you for jobs based on your reputation? If you own a business, how many new clients are you getting from referrals? Did you know that sixty-five percent of all new business comes from referrals? Are you in an industry leadership position where you are being sought after for media interviews? Are your colleagues, clients, or bosses talking about how well you get the job done? Have any of them made an unsolicited recommendation on your behalf? Aside from your organic reputation dividends from the above, another way to increase awareness or build up your reputation account is to purposely harness the power of online social media outlets. Job networking sites such as LinkedIn offer opportunities and encourage people to leave feedback or recommendations for you and your work. An easy first step is to assess how many recommendations you have. Or in the spirit of helping others, think about how many recommendations you have made for others. Identify the people who would be good candidates to leave feedback on not only your work, but also how you worked with them, how you led a team, how you handled yourself during a tough situation. These are all indicators and foundation stones for your reputation. So, don't be afraid to first ask for a recommendation, but also ask for specific feedback that helps shape the story you want others to read about you and thus continue to build your personal reputation account. This will take effort and follow through, but if you use technology to your advantage, you can generate the groundswell to shape, build, and maintain your reputation.

Social media communities built around personal or professional interests are great outlets to connect with people and a way to not only grow, but to strengthen your network and increase your influence. These channels keep you relevant, engaged, and, most of all, aware of what's going on around you so that you can be a participant rather than just a spectator.

Remember, your reputation transcends your job title, your revenues, your job responsibilities, and, if applicable, your current job search. It precedes you as well as follows you, for better or worse. Try not to approach managing and building your reputation as a daily chore. Rather, it's an investment in you, a responsibility in which you should take great interest. You are the president of the Bank of You, and the bank is always open.

SHIFT POINTS:

- Your reputation is a form of currency and can be more valuable than money

- Reputations build credibility and authenticity for leaders, which can help them achieve goals or rally a team

- Reputations can open doors for opportunities

- Strong reputations allow leaders opportunities for second chances

- Building up a strong reputation "balance" is a daily endeavor and is strengthened by your decisions and actions over time

ACCELERATION:

1. List five ways in which your reputation is more valuable than money.

    1. _____
    2. _____
    3. _____
    4. _____
    5. _____

2. Write down a time when your reputation helped you get the results you needed. Maybe it was a job, a new piece of business, perhaps even forgiveness and a second chance.

    _____

    _____

3. Circle the phrase that best captures how often your reputation has generated opportunities for you.

    Very Frequently (1–2X per month)   Frequently (1–2X every 6 months)

    Not Frequently (1X or fewer per year)

    . . . Now list three things you can do to enhance your reputation.

    REPUTATION ENHANCEMENT 1

    _____

    _____

    REPUTATION ENHANCEMENT 2

    _____

    _____

REPUTATION ENHANCEMENT 3

_____

_____

4. Write down two instances in your life when you gave someone a second chance because of their reputation.

RE-DO 1

_____

_____

RE-DO 2

_____

_____

5. What are five actions or decisions you have made over the last six months that have increased your Bank of You balance?

BANK OF YOU INCREASE 1

_____

_____

BANK OF YOU INCREASE 2

_____

_____

BANK OF YOU INCREASE 3

_____

_____

BANK OF YOU INCREASE 4

_____

_____

Chapter Three

TRUTH NUMBER 2:
KNOW WHAT'S BEING SAID ABOUT YOU
Japanese Drivers and Reputation Spotters

*The way to gain a good reputation is to endeavor
to be what you desire to appear.*
—*Socrates, Greek Philosopher*

"*I*nside. Inside. Two more. Inside. Clear. You're clear to move up.*" That is the voice of one of the most important people in NASCAR racing—the spotter.

Naturally, when we think of the key players on a race team, our thoughts go to the driver, whose role is pretty self-explanatory. The crew chief, who is responsible for the team's race strategy and translating the driver's feedback about the handling of the car into actionable steps for the pit crew during a pit stop as well as gathering and digesting information from numerous team engineers, is another crucial member of the team. And, of course, there is the pit crew, whose collective responsibility is to service the car as quickly as possible during each pit stop.

However, the spotter is an almost invisible team position, though it is one of the most critical when it comes to a team's success on the racetrack.

If you have ever been to a NASCAR race and listened to the team communications on a radio scanner, you've heard the spotter as an anonymous voice. Unlike the rest of the team, who work closely with the driver and car on pit road, the spotter does his job far from the team and is only linked to them by radio transmission from a roof high atop the track facility where he has a clear view of every area on the racetrack. You see, the spotter is essentially the driver's eyes in the sky, helping the driver safely navigate 200 mile-per-hour machines through every race. They are the only person who can see a driver's blind spots, the small areas around the car, that are often measured in only inches, that the driver's mirrors just can't show. They are the voices that deftly guides the drivers through the smoke and wreckage of a multicar pileup in order to come through it unscathed.

The relationship between a spotter and driver is unique. Longevity, communication, and trust are the hallmarks of these relationships. The good ones know their driver's driving style so well and have logged so many hundreds of hours in their perch that they know the competition's idiosyncrasies, too. Based on the situation, a spotter can anticipate what both his driver and the competition will do and help the driver "see" what is about to unfold around them. The implicit trust that a driver puts in a spotter cannot be understated—consider that a mistake in a spotter's verbal guidance can cause a multicar wreck if he's not in the moment and concentrating on what his driver is doing and what those around him are trying to do.

Horsepower in the Land of the Rising Sun

In 2002, I was a partner at a motorsports marketing, advertising, and public relations agency, Cox Group, which helped introduce the first Japanese NASCAR driver to the sport on American soil, or more specifically, American asphalt. Team owner Travis Carter fielded Hideo Fukuyama (pronounced "Hih-day-o") in 1996 and 1997 when NASCAR held exhibition races at Suzuka Circuit, a renowned road course in Japan. Fukuyama was an Eastern driving sensation who primarily raced sports cars, having won numerous races including the prestigious 24 Hours of Le Mans endurance race in 2000 while driving in the GT3 class. It was during the exhibition events in Japan that he caught the eye of NASCAR legend Dale Earnhardt. Earnhardt encouraged Fukuyama to pursue his dream of racing stock cars full time in America.

It was at that point when Travis and Earnhardt discussed plans that could make Hideo the first Japanese full-time driver in NASCAR.

The Suzuka native was affable and fun-loving, didn't have a large entourage, and was very low maintenance. He could understand English well and spoke some broken English, but we knew that we would have some language barriers on the public relations and marketing side of the operation. To get ahead of that, my partners, Rodrick and Doug Cox decided to find someone who could speak, write, and translate Japanese fluently. That individual would not only serve as Hideo's public relations manager but also support the race team however they could when it came to communicating. This racing business is hard enough even when everyone on the team speaks the same language!

While we searched through résumés, Hideo and the rest of us continued to communicate in a manner that looked more like a game of charades than meaningful conversation. There were a lot of hand gestures, drawings on paper, and pointing at the race car to try and make certain points. We learned that there were few perfect or pure translations of racing terms.

We all did our best to learn key racing phrases in Japanese, and he did the same in English, which worked well when we were face to face. But it was far from perfect once Hideo strapped on his helmet and the conversation left the world of visual gestures.

After finding and hiring a great young lady, Samantha Switzer—out of Asheville, North Carolina, of all places (the Appalachian Mountains was not where I would have thought we would find someone with those specific skills!)—we quickly got her immersed with the team and had her involved in meetings. She started working with Hideo, Travis, the crew chief, and the spotter on finding some "bridge" words and phrases that would cross the language gap.

After numerous on-track test and communications sessions with driver, team owner, crew, chief, and spotter it was time for the No. 66 Ford to take to the track.

Hideo would attempt to qualify for the NASCAR Sprint Cup Series race at the Monster Mile at Dover International Speedway just outside of Wilmington, Delaware. If he qualified, he would become the first Japanese driver to race in a NASCAR points event.

Hideo's passion, commitment, and respect for Earnhardt was conveyed in an interview he did with a writer for the Associated Press prior the race. "I am here to keep a promise to the late Mr. Dale Earnhardt," he said.

Travis knew what this meant on a personal level to Hideo,

who was responsible not only for his own ambitions, but also those of his family and country. Travis was always impressed by Hideo's approach and his ability to learn.

"I was impressed with Hideo when he drove for me in Japan and continue to be impressed with his ability to adapt and drive these race cars," Travis said in an interview. "He's very methodical and thinks things through. He understands more words than he can speak and we've worked on specific words and what they mean."

Forty-six cars were vying for forty-three starting positions, and Hideo claimed the last and final slot to qualify as the first Japanese driver to race in NASCAR's top series.

The spotter and Hideo spent a significant period of time together and went through the various phrases and sayings to ensure that in the heat of battle the driver would always know what was happening around him.

The green flag waved to start the MBNA All-American Heroes 400, and Hideo drove a car adorned with an American-and-Japanese-flag paint scheme and the words "Standing Together" across the hood. He did well to keep himself out of trouble in the early stages of the 400-mile race. It wasn't long into the race that he was lapped by the leaders, which was one of the first true tests of how well the spotter and Hideo would communicate and work together.

While the spotter and Hideo worked very well together during the race, what wasn't working was the car's transmission, which eventually was the cause of Hideo's day ending on lap 243. He finished thirty-ninth but still had a huge smile on his face. I'm sure he was hiding some disappointment, but he seemed like he was just living in the moment of what he and the team had accomplished.

REPUTATION SPOTTERS

How would life be different if we had spotters? Imagine if we had people in our lives who were able to see our blind spots. Or hold you accountable for decisions you've made. Or reach out when they see something out of character. Think of them as Reputation Spotters.

The reality is that we all do have Reputation Spotters in our lives, but we rarely engage them. But in today's Reputation Economy, we can't afford to overlook resources or, more importantly, not be open to feedback.

One morning after a workout, I got back to my car and checked my phone only to find a text from a friend of mine, Jeff Smith, saying, "Bro—I know you are pissed (no clue what for) but be careful on social media. Folks troll that stuff like crazy. Looking out for you . . . don't want you to get railroaded! Hope everything is OK . . . let me know."

Immediately, my mind started racing about what I may have posted that might have been taken out of context and wondering if one of my social channels had been hacked since I didn't recall posting anything that could get me "railroaded." After a quick back and forth with Jeff, it turned out that the issue was with a different friend with the same last name. OK, huge relief for me that it was only a mistake on Jeff's end, but his gesture and genuine concern was important, nonetheless.

YOUR REPUTATION AUDIT

Knowing that we have people in our lives who have our "social" backs can be invaluable in keeping us in check with what we do or share online. But, remember the old saying "your reputation precedes you"? Do you know what your reputation is?

Ever thought about it, or asked someone? For many, the answer is no. Or, they have an idea of what their reputation based on what they want it to be. However, in this ever competitive world, where opportunities can pass you by because of just one person's experiences with you, you can't afford not to know or have an objective idea of what your reputation might be.

To do this takes planning, commitment, and courage.

Let's put this in perspective. For a moment, think about the amount of time you spend preparing for and working through planning and strategy sessions and creating PowerPoint decks or forecast spreadsheets for your business or clients.

How many hours would you estimate you *spend* in these planning endeavors?

A study performed by Financial Executives Research Foundation to determine what it costs companies to develop annual plans estimated that employees spend 10.5 days on annual business planning. While that does not take into account quarterly updates or other business-plan revisions, easy math shows we spend an average of eighty-four hours on this process—and that is just an estimate!

But what often gets lost in the throes of corporate brand planning is your personal brand planning. Your product is your reputation.

So again I ask, how many hours do you *invest* in critically thinking about your reputation? I'll make a leap and assume it's less than the time you spend in business planning—safe bet, right?

Remember the ZMOT theory from earlier? That is the critical moment when people are searching for answers, shopper feedback, and insights that will lead them to a purchasing decision. I ask you to think about how that applies when assessing personal reputations, perhaps when people are making hiring decisions or looking for personnel resources. Think about a time when you spoke with an industry friend who said that they were looking at a few candidates and wanted your feedback about a particular person. As I wrote earlier, your frame of reference on this person is usually based on a blend of two things. The first is what you have experienced yourself, which could have been either a positive or negative outcome. The second is based on what you have heard from others about the candidate—essentially, the person's reputation.

So, how would you fare in the scenario above if you were the candidate someone was asking about? The truth is that you probably wouldn't even know.

A Reputation Audit is your opportunity to get hands on and invest in yourself and your future. It may sound overwhelming, scary, boring, even ridiculous or some combination of those.

I challenge you, urge you, dare you to take this first step in planning, honing, and owning your personal brand.

Dave Logan, best-selling author and management consultant, wrote a great article for CBS MoneyWatch regarding the value and importance of conducting a Personal Reputation Audit.

"The biggest lesson I've learned in twenty years of consulting is that leaders need to know what others are saying about them, or risk losing their job," Logan wrote. Knowing what people are saying about you doesn't just apply for those in C-level positions. It also matters for those who aspire to grow professionally and personally during this journey in life.

TRUST, TRANSPARENCY, AND WOM

Have you ever been in a situation when someone you know to have a less than stellar reputation in their industry or company tells you how shocked they were that they didn't get the promotion? And while you are externally nodding your head in disbelief as they recount this to you, internally, you are shaking your head and raising an eyebrow as if to say, "no kidding?" Has that ever happened to you? Or, perhaps you had a friend tell you a similar story about a mutual connection, and you weren't surprised because you have your own impression of them and know what others say or think about them.

Referrals are one of the best reputation barometers in existence. Essentially, a referral is someone else putting their reputation on the line for an individual or a company. The value of that type of personal, word of mouth (WOM) affirmation to a business owner cannot be underestimated. Remember the earlier statistic I shared? Sixty-five percent of new business comes from referrals.

The rise of consumer-feedback sites like Angie's List, Yelp, and Yik Yak can either put your business into referral overdrive or leave your business stuck in neutral, worse yet, without new referrals you could be out of business.

Author, entrepreneur, and consultant, John Jantsch, who created the Duct Tape Marketing empire and has written the best-selling book *The Referral Engine*, asserts that trust is one of the pillars of referrals. In his Duct Tape Marketing blog post titled "60 Ways to Screw Up the Customer Experience," Jantsch highlights the power of trust and how it is inextricably connected to our reputations—either as business owners or individuals.

"No one buys from companies they do not trust and it's never been easier to learn who is trustworthy, and who is not," Jantsch writes. "We don't do business with companies that even total strangers have told us don't keep their word. Proactively managing your reputation online and off has to be part of the marketing puzzle."

Can you think of a time when a colleague said that she was looking for an agency to help with a specific project and asked for a referral and your opinion?

At this point, you begin to mentally assess the agency options based on either your personal, firsthand experiences, or third-party feedback from people you trust, which is essentially WOM reputation. Your firsthand feedback could have been based on a number of factors, such as the agency's ability to manage a budget, creative problem-solving techniques, or the quality of its work product. You more than likely also evaluated the agency by the individuals with whom you worked or interacted. Perhaps you also thought about their attitudes, their work process, and their ability to exceed expectations and meet deadlines?

After quickly processing all of that or even sharing your experiences with your colleague, your answer may have gone something like this, "I worked with that agency before and I can tell you that the product they developed for me was great, but it was a nightmare working with their account team. They constantly blew deadlines and it took three days to get any type of reply to my emails. They have that reputation for delivering good work, but it takes longer than expected and the people don't make it an enjoyable experience."

Or have you ever heard or given this answer? "I've been satisfied with the work they do, but wouldn't work with that agency as long as Bob is there. He's arrogant and I don't fully trust him. He's not proactive at all and can be disrespectful in meetings and it's clear that his colleagues don't respect him by what they say about him."

What if you owned the agency where Bob worked? You'd have no idea how much referral business you were losing because of what people thought of him—his reputation. Beyond the business owner's perspective, what if you were Bob? Do you know that your reputation is hindering your career? More than likely, the answer would be no for both questions because rarely, if ever, does that kind of feedback make its way back to either the agency owner or Bob. Clients will often move on. Now, I have experienced as you may have, too, a client sharing negative feedback with senior executives or the agency owner who have then either reassigned Bob or let him go from the agency in order to save the business. But that only happens if there is a high level of trust and transparency in the communication and relationship—you've still got to know that another Bob won't be put on the account.

As you can see, whether you are losing referral business or career opportunities, it all relates back to reputations. There has never been another time in human history when there have been so many choices and ways to search for options, whether those are new business, jobs, products, or services. Remember the Bank of You message from the earlier chapter? Referrals are like social collateral from your or other people's banks. The person making the referral is essentially drawing against their "bank account," because its value is based on the experiences they have had with you and their willingness to use their reputations as a kind of collateral.

STYLE IS EVERYTHING

If you are a business owner or entrepreneur, you understand that your company's reputation not only rests on the blood, sweat, and tears you have invested and continue to invest, but also on the daily actions, interactions, and decisions of your employees. They are either building or tarnishing your company's reputation with each engagement with customers, vendors, and prospects. If you do have a team of people working for you, I would consider them all reputation ambassadors for you and your company.

This is the value of a Reputation Audit. It allows you to be proactive about the reputation halo that is around you. This is true not only for organizations and their people, but also for us as individuals.

Logan has an interesting perspective. He goes on to write that, "your reputation is about you, but it isn't your property. It's owned by the tribe around you. So when you ask about your reputation, odd as it may seem, you're asking about something that isn't yours. Getting any information about your reputation relies on the goodwill and generosity of others."

The way you approach this conversation is also critical. Don't come at this exercise as if there is something terminally wrong, you're worked up into a frenzy, or you're on a quest for some deep and magical truth. A Personal Reputation Audit is just one tool that you can use in an overall effort to assess, gauge, build, or rehabilitate your reputation, not a magic bullet.

Logan offers a similar approach for when you are ready to launch your audit. "This is an important process. If you approach it like something is terribly wrong, or this is your self-development idea of the day, it may harm the reputation you're trying to assess. When cool people do a reputation audit, it helps their reputation. So be cool about it."

There are several ways of conducting a Personal Reputation Audit. The first is doing an online search to see what surfaces about you. This could be done assessing what you find on professional social networking sites like LinkedIn to see if people are endorsing your skills or not. The second is the one that requires the courage I mentioned earlier. This is done through face-to-face conversations with others. This is the place where you will more than likely get uncomfortable and where a majority of people will stop and not take the step forward. However, if you invest the time, approach it with an open mind, and connect with the right people, I can promise you that this exercise will change the way you view your reputation!

Below are seven steps to approaching a Personal Reputation Audit.

1. Identify a core group of people who you know well and trust or whose insight you respect—these are your personal Reputation Spotters. We are multidimensional people, and we need to gain a multidimensional perspective on our reputation. In a way, our reputations are sort of like mosaics instead of one crisp image. That is why it's important to identify a wide range of colleagues, clients, friends, or family who know you and have seen you in different areas of your life. Consider people who have known you for various periods of time—a lifetime or a few months. This type of mix is ideal to gain a broad sense of your reputation and also to find out if there are consistencies or inconsistencies as it relates to how you've interacted with different groups of people. I want to stress that these need to be people you trust and who you believe will give you honest feedback. This is key to building your reputational awareness.

2. Explain what you are trying to get out of this exercise and ask if they would be willing to help you. You can even use the racing spotter analogy to help illustrate why you need their input and feedback. You need someone who can see your blind spots. Let them know that you need honest, objective answers about what they *see* and *hear* as it relates to your reputation.

Keep in mind that you aren't asking them to give you *their* opinion of your reputation. You should understand that this might be difficult for some people to do and could make them uncomfortable. Remember that human nature has us wired to avoid situations that could cause us pain or discomfort, whether that is physical, emotional, or psychological. And if these are close friends, colleagues, or even clients, you want to assure them that there will be no retribution or relationship issues between you as a result of the conversation—encourage transparency. Also, recognize that most people want to make us feel good, so they may focus on the positives. My hope is that you would get that positive feedback, which is very important for reinforcement purposes. But, let's look at ourselves in the mirror and recognize that none of us is perfect, right? So, you should also get some constructive direction, too, which will then allow you to begin the proper course correction.

3. Remember that reputations are not typically built upon objective accounts. Rather, they are often filtered, subjectively, either by a first person's account based on their view of the situation or through second and third parties based on what they've heard through someone else's filter. Here's a simple way to think through this: Take a moment and recall a time when you and a colleague or friend were remembering a situation. It could be either a fun memory of a night out or perhaps dissecting a tense company meeting. Do you remember a point in the conversation with your friend when you realized that you missed a detail of the story that they told you about that made the experience even funnier? It happens sometimes since we miss details, because of our perspective, that put the whole picture together. Or, if the person you were talking to is a colleague and you both were discussing how you saw that contentious meeting unfolding, you might have stopped and said, "No, that's not what I meant at all when I said that." This scenario often happens because people digest what they hear and see through their own set of filters, which truthfully aren't always rational or mature filters! As frustrating as that may be, it is reality, and it speaks to the importance of weaving a consistent thread of actions that are in accordance with your personal values.

4. Don't react or try to defend yourself from the observations they share or the feedback they give. If your Reputation Spotters begin to sense that you are getting defensive, they will naturally begin dialing back the feedback they are sharing with you. After all, they didn't accept your invitation to coffee, lunch, or a beer to get into an argument or have to defend what they've heard or experienced. Be respectful of what you say in response to their comments. In fact, try not to say anything other than "thank you for being honest and helping me." Beyond what you say, be mindful of your body language, too. Our body language will speak more honestly and clearly than any words we can push out of our mouths.

According to Public Words, a great resource created by Dr. Nick Morgan who is an author and communications coach for celebrities, executives, and athletes, humans can produce more than 250,000 facial expressions and more than a thousand physical postures. Think about that and the depth of your vocabulary! In 1967, a researcher named Albert Mehrabian was studying the importance of verbal and nonverbal communications channels. It was after this study that he developed the 55/38/7 formula that represented the percentages of how individuals communicate—55 percent of communication is done through body language, 38 percent is the tone in the person's voice, and 7 percent represents the actual words that are spoken.

Be mindful of the messages you are conveying even when you are not speaking.

5. Take notes so you can reflect on the feedback later and see if there are any themes or trends that begin to surface. This is important for a number of reasons. You will hopefully be getting a lot of feedback. It will be natural to replay the conversations in your head at a later date, but at that point you don't want to rely solely on your memory. Also, the fact that you identified Reputation Spotters from various aspects of your life will allow you to gather a wider view and give you broader insights.

Consider organizing your notes by the different people in your life and the ways you interact with them. For example, the categories could be "Work," "Family," "Friends", and "Community." By looking at your notes and the trends or themes that emerge, you may be able to see what behaviors or perceptions appear more consistently. This will allow you to focus your energy and attention in specific areas of your life or recognize where your actions and decisions weren't holistically congruent.

6. Sincerely thank them for their honesty since there is some inherent risk in this type of exercise—for them as well as yourself. Being present and in the moment, just as NASCAR spotters must be, is one of the greatest gifts we can give another person. It's the gift of our time, attention, and respect. These are precious resources that don't seem to be in ample supply these days when all it takes is a buzz from a smartphone to bring a conversation to a halt in order to see what someone else has to say or what notification your favorite app has delivered. This audit is an investment in you and your future—both personally and professionally. And, by your Reputation Spotters being honest, they are also investing in you and your relationship with them. So thank them for having the courage to get uncomfortable with you—we never grow in the status quo! Who knows, maybe they will ask you to return the favor?

7. Digest the feedback and develop an action plan based on specific areas of your reputation that you want to correct or even enhance. An exercise this specific and personal would be a complete waste of your and your Reputation Spotter's time if you didn't develop an action plan. The fact that you would initiate a Personal Reputation Audit would lead me to believe that you are serious about enhancing your reputation and making it work harder for you in this Reputation Economy.

Here's an important step. Before you start going through all of your notes and begin to think through your action plan, pause for a moment and just think of the person you are and the reputation you want to have *earned*.

Don't just think about the person you are today, but more importantly, the person you want to be. Once you have a clear vision of that person, write it down. Once you have done that, think about the values that person possesses and the types of behaviors and decisions they would make. I don't mean that you should pretend or change who you are, it's really about enhancing what you have and harnessing your potential.

You see, it is important to recognize that reputations can evolve as we mature or go through different life experiences. What you have done is shed light in areas of your life that will require daily attention and consistent focus over a long period of time.

Now that you have the feedback from your Reputation Spotters and a clear self-vision, you can begin to create your action steps—small steps that you can make on a consistent basis to begin evolving your reputation. One bit of advice—don't try to change, develop, or enhance everything at once. Look at your list and begin to prioritize what areas need your attention before moving on to the other audit points on your list. For example, in your "Work" category, are there consistent themes of unresponsiveness, or not actively participating in client meetings? Those would be two immediate areas where you could have a positive impact on with daily and deliberate actions.

Also, while it is human nature to focus on negative feedback, take the time to build upon your positive attributes, too. This intent of this audit is not for it to be a personal beat down, rather it should serve as a source of empowerment. Find that balance to improve your strengths and strengthen your weaknesses. Put your actions into play on a consistent basis and you will realize how, over time, your reputation improves. You'll be able to not only see but also reap its benefits in all aspects of your life.

SHIFT POINTS:

- Leaders need people in their lives who will tell them what they need to hear, not what they want to hear

- Leaders are neither able to reinforce the good nor identify and fix the bad if they live in a vacuum and don't know or listen to what is being said about them

- Referrals are a powerful indicator as to the health and value of a leader's reputation

- When leading, people watch your feet, not your mouth—actions speak louder than words

Acceleration:

1. List five people in your life who will tell you what you *need* to hear, not what you *want* to hear.
   1. _____
   2. _____
   3. _____
   4. _____
   5. _____

2. What are the five words you want to hear in your reputation audit?
   1. _____
   2. _____
   3. _____
   4. _____
   5. _____

3. On a scale of 1–5 (1 being not frequently and 5 being very frequently) how often do you seek out personal and professional feedback?

   1   2   3   4   5

4. Finish the sentence, "When I get feedback, I hear …"

   _____

5. List five ways you have built trust among friends, family, colleagues and clients over the past 30 days.

   Trust Point 1. _____
   Trust Point 2. _____
   Trust Point 3. _____
   Trust Point 4. _____
   Trust Point 5. _____

6. On a scale of 1–5 (1 being not aligned and 5 being very aligned) how would your closest friends, customers or colleagues rate how your actions align with your words.

1   2   3   4   5

Chapter Four

TRUTH NUMBER 3:
SUMMING UP YOUR REPUTATION EQUATION

"Smoke 'em if you got 'em."

*The most important thing for a young man is to
establish credit—a reputation and character.*
—John D. Rockefeller, Entrepreneur

WHILE AMERICANS WONDERED IF WE WOULD AWAKE to technological darkness during the Y2K hysteria in mid-1999, the government was moving forward with its efforts to limit the ways
in which tobacco companies could promote sports sponsorships
and market to consumers. For an industry that invested signifi-
cantly in sports, this type of legislation would make it harder for
tobacco brands to engage with consumers, build commercially
driven brand equity, and sample its products. For NASCAR and
series sponsor R. J. Reynolds, whose relationship spanned more
than three decades, all signs indicated that they were nearing
their last drag together.

Tobacco is a pretty polarizing product. People either like it or hate it—there is rarely any middle ground in terms of public sentiment. However, R. J. Reynolds and specifically its Winston brand spent hundreds of millions of dollars to not only support and promote the NASCAR Winston Cup Series, but it also helped build and maintain many race facilities and brought an aggressive and fan-oriented marketing acumen to a league whose primary focus had been purely competition. So, in a sport that is renowned for its fan loyalty toward its sponsors, Winston actually had a very positive reputation, even among non-smokers, not for what it made (tobacco products), but for what it helped make better (NASCAR racing).

To its credit, as stewards of one of the most high-profile sports in the world, the executives at R. J. Reynolds gave the top brass at NASCAR the green light to begin a search for a new series sponsor in 2001. The verbal agreement was that Winston would remain as the series sponsor as long as the government would allow, based on pending legislation, or until NASCAR could secure another corporation to assume its role.

ANSWERING THE CALL

On June 18, 2003 an announcement between NASCAR and Nextel Communications was made in New York City. R. J. Reynolds's partnership with NASCAR was extinguished after thirty-three years. Regardless of your stance on tobacco, the people at R. J. Reynolds looked at their role in the sport as a partnership. These were people, such as the late T. Wayne Robertson, who were interwoven into the fabric of the sport—they weighed in on competitive decisions and had personal relationships with NASCAR executives, drivers, track promoters, fans, and their families. Winston had developed an incredibly strong reputation as not just a stakeholder or sponsor, but as an advocate for the sport, the drivers, and fans. This was not a traditional sponsorship by any stretch of the imagination.

Tim Donahue, Tom Kelly, and Mark Schweitzer, at the time Nextel's CEO, COO, and CMO, respectively, had been the men to get board approval of what was reportedly a ten-year, $750-million sponsorship—at the time, the largest in all of professional sports. These men knew they'd have to approach this long-term sponsorship in a way that was first and foremost about doing the right things for the sport and its fans. NASCAR boasts a fan base of seventy-five million who are known to reward its sponsors by purchasing their products over non-sponsor products by a ratio, according to independent studies, of three to one.

While there was relief within NASCAR's offices that a mainstream corporation like a wireless telecommunications company had signed on, there was a great deal of unrest among the legions of fans who thought that the world of NASCAR racing was about to get turned on its head. While we all knew that the sport's on-track product would still be the same as it had been for decades, there was genuine concern among fans that wondered if Nextel had "just stroked a check," or if there was real commitment to "their" sport. I can't blame them for that. Honestly, they didn't know Nextel's intentions, and more importantly, what it was going to do in NASCAR. Online message boards and forums were racing with negative threads about the many ways Nextel was going to ruin the sport because they weren't fans and they had no connection to racing—it was just about selling phones. Some fans went so far as to create and post faux corporate logos such as "Next-Hell." For the Nextel executives, this outpouring of opinions and emotions not only further punctuated the passion of NASCAR fans but also took away any safety net they might have—they knew it had to be done right.

I was fortunate to be recruited to be part of a small team of people who mapped out how the NASCAR Nextel Cup Series sponsorship would come to life. Our focus and purpose was to choreograph how Nextel would integrate its technology into NASCAR racing to bring fans closer to the sport they loved, truly enhance the at-track communications experience, and transcend pure sponsorship to being a true partner and demonstrating that we too were fans. We knew that consistent behaviors based on our values would build our reputation and establish a level of trust among the core constituents—fans, drivers, track and media partners, as well as NASCAR and the many other sponsors that support the industry. When you think about it, those are a lot of masters to serve, but that mindset became the foundation of our everyday actions and strategic plans.

HIRING FROM WITHIN

Nextel was very smart in its hiring strategy for its launch team. They handpicked people who were well known within the NASCAR community and had been in the industry for many years, some even former R. J. Reynolds staff. The thinking was very simple, yet leveraged a very important element for building and managing reputations—it's called the halo effect of association. The message to the industry and fans was this, "You may not know Nextel, but you know and trust these people. Give us a chance to show you what we can do together." Nextel traded off the reputations of the people who were established in the sport by bringing them on to the corporate team to instill trust and ensure credibility among the industry stakeholders, opinion leaders, and fans. Then, based on our track records, we would deliver results to continue enhancing and strengthening Nextel's position within the sport. The result of that plan coming together would be a less dramatic learning curve when bringing the sponsorship to life, immediate trust, and credibility for the core corporate team among industry stakeholders, which then built a stronger reputation for the series sponsor.

My primary focus was to lead public and media relations as well as marketing communications initiatives for the sponsorship. Those responsibilities ranged from strategically launching new technology products for fans and writing speeches for executives to developing a multitude of crisis plans and ensuring that our values aligned with our actions as the series sponsor. We all worked at a head-spinning rate. Considering what we were walking into, it was a huge task that truly was a double-edged sword. On one side, we had a clean slate to work with and could mold the reputation we so desired. On the other side, people were waiting for us to trip up so they could say, "I told you they would mess it up. Winston wouldn't have done that!"

WALKING IN WINSTON'S SHADOW

It was November 6, 2003, and the core Nextel team all went to the last race of the Winston Cup era at Homestead-Miami Speedway. It was an opportunity for us to talk with our industry partners and share a few ideas and initiatives for 2004 in an attempt to soothe some uncertainty.

Come February, we came out of the gates strong and hit the ground running, but not without having to wrestle with Winston's shadow. Those two words, "Winston's shadow," are not mine. The late David Poole, a good friend and veteran motorsports writer for the *Charlotte Observer*, used those words when we were talking at Homestead-Miami Speedway the morning of that final Winston Cup race. He told me not to take things too personally when the media and fans attacked us. Essentially, he said, every move would be critiqued; every word and quote scrutinized against what Winston had or would have done. He went on to say that nothing would ever seem to be enough because we would be walking in Winston's shadow for some time—and he was right. I always appreciated David's brutal honesty and perspectives on life and the sport. If you think about David's words, they could be applied to any of us, in my opinion. Have you ever been in a position where people were watching how you would handle a situation? Perhaps you took over a position for someone who left the company that was truly admired and respected—filling those big shoes isn't always easy under a microscope!

We were successful in bringing this sponsorship to life in a way that was authentic to the sport, the fan base, and our brand. We worked tirelessly to gain the confidence of the NASCAR industry and its fans by deliberately charting out our path and sticking to our core messages—we are fans of NASCAR; we respect the heritage and history of the sport; we only want to enhance the experience through our technology—then actively and passionately backing those up with our consistent actions and behaviors.

Actively managing your reputation takes the same mental outlook and approach—it cannot be viewed as a task or a "to-do" on a checklist. While it may sound a bit militant, actively managing your reputation must be a way of life because every action will dictate a positive or negative outcome.

The Reputation Equation

Math was never my strongest subject in school. In fact, we often celebrated in our house when I brought home a C. While it's a subject that I had to fight through, I did learn that to answer a mathematical question, regardless of its complexity, you must break it down into a manageable equation. This will allow you to see how each element works in an effort to prove the answer.

Think of actively managing your reputation in a similar fashion. By breaking it down into an equation you will easily see what elements build out a reputation. I created the Reputation Equation as a simple visual image to do just that. It is built upon the formula that our values influence our decisions, our decisions drive our behavior, and our consistent behavior, over time, becomes our reputation.

It looks like this: Values + Decisions + Behavior + Time = Reputation.

The purpose of the Reputation Equation is to visually shift your view of how to manage your reputation in this new economy where reputations are the currency. Traditionally, public relations professionals will work with clients (either personalities or corporations) to understand what their objectives are (essentially what they want to get done) then identify their values and begin to choreograph strategic events or stories that with authenticity, consistency, and time, will begin to positively shift or influence public opinions and perceptions. That's a very boiled down explanation of a demanding craft that takes years to hone. In my opinion, it all starts with values because that's the authentic link between what someone stands for and what their actions back up.

Living What You Believe

In order to dial up your awareness of your personal reputation management, you must focus on the words to the left of the equal sign, regardless of whether you are leading a Fortune 100 corporation, starting your own franchise, managing your small business, or continuing down a path of self-improvement as an individual. Such perspective allows you to become more actively engaged in the steps that lead to how your reputation is built, protected, and managed.

Take a minute and think of someone who has come into your life or who you have observed that you would say lives with conviction and authenticity. Someone who you look at and can say they not only "talk the talk" but, more importantly, "walk the walk."

These people do exist; they could be your pastor, boss, friend, doctor, accountant, or spouse. And, if you ask them how they do it, I'm sure that the answer would contain three important components. First, they would say that they are intimately aware of what is important to them—honesty, integrity, fairness, forgiveness, loyalty, humor . . . the list could go on and on. They have invested the time to create an unobstructed view of their values and are deliberately living them out to others in a way that not only makes us admire and respect them, but also strengthens their reputations.

The second part of their answer is that it's not easy living out your values. We don't live in a perfect world where everything lines up in accordance with what we believe.

And the third is that they do their best to make the best decisions and act accordingly every day. While none of us is perfect, it's the deliberate decision to get up and do our best each and every day that will always separate those who do from those who want to.

Let's look at this thought from a different perspective. You could say that by living without the conscious thoughts of our values and how we bring them to life, we are essentially disconnected from them and may never fully recognize our true potential.

VALUES

So, take a step back and think about your values. Take some time to think about those guiding principles in your life, the things that are important to you. Do words like honesty and integrity come to mind? How about reliable or curiosity? Why do these words matter to you? What is it about these values that when put together begin to create a representation of you? There's an old saying among savvy consumers, "everything is negotiable." We hear it often, especially in the current buyers' market in which we are living. So, again, take a step back and determine if your values are negotiable. They shouldn't be. However, much like an exercise regimen, it takes mental strength, commitment, and endurance in order to see your results—building your reputation based upon your values is much the same.

There's no doubt that life would be easier to get through if we didn't have to consider our reputations, or if they were stored neatly in a box. The reality is that no reputation is just sitting idle or dormant. It's quite the opposite. Your reputation is a living testament to who you are and what you do and is on display twenty-four hours a day, seven days a week, 365 days a year. It doesn't matter if you are introverted or extroverted, a polished executive or green intern, we are all accountable.

The too often reported and sad reality is that many in our society have become ignorant of their reputation's value and shrug off their personal responsibility and accountability when it comes to the outcomes of their actions.

Don't believe me? Think back to some of the previous stories I've shared in this book. Or, read the headlines, listen to the radio, and spend some time on social media channels and you'll see clear examples of why, now more than ever, we all have to proactively protect and manage our reputations by shifting our level of awareness, accountability, and responsibility. This all starts with what we consciously and consistently value!

DECISIONS. DECISIONS. DECISIONS.

According to various online studies, the average person makes thirty-five thousand decisions a day. Those range from the mundane—when to brush your teeth and which alternate route you should take to work because of construction—all the way up to critical and strategic decisions at work. Sounds like a lot, right? A study from Cornell University researchers found that we make an average of more than 220 decisions about just food each day! Decisions are difficult to dissect because of the variety of both internal and external influences and considerations through which we must filter them. Think about a decision you recently made where you had to factor in internal elements such as your emotions, past experiences, and intuition as well as external circumstances such as work or home environment and culture, expectations, and potential consequences. You are probably thinking to yourself, "Yeah, that's just about every decision I make." I was thinking the same thing. Now, let me ask you, during some of those big decisions when did you have to factor in your values? Did that make the decision more difficult? Perhaps it made the decision more clear? In some cases, people will rationalize their way to a decision. Ever done that? I know I have. Statements such as "well I've worked hard for this" and "it's just this one time." Have you ever heard something like "no one is really going to know" or "it's not going to hurt anyone"? In some psychology circles, rationalization is considered a defense mechanism where people try to justify or explain negative or controversial behaviors or thoughts into understandable terms. Often we find that the easy decision is not always aligned with our values. Sometimes it's a matter of people just being plain stubborn when it comes to making decisions! It's not a matter of a good idea or the necessity to see a different perspective—it's a situation when a person has just dug in their heels because it's "different" or "challenges the status quo." Have you ever had experiences with a person like that?

Remember a company named Kodak? George Eastman created the photography company in 1878 at a time when photographs were still taken with wet plates. He was one of the first innovators of the time and made a move toward dry plates, which were more convenient and easier to use than their predecessor. Kodak was also the first company to move from dry plates to film and later was the first to introduce color film. So, at its core, this was a company that understood the value, impact, and necessity of evolution and innovation. Did you know that a Kodak engineer named Steve Sasson created the first digital camera and presented it to corporate executives in 1975? According to an interview Sasson did with the *New York Times*, his bosses were not impressed with his invention and despite his arguments of how the landscape of photography could change, "They were convinced that no one would ever want to look at their pictures on a television set." Kodak launched its first digital camera in 1995, but since its business was built around film and printing, it never fully committed—it dabbled. When Kodak finally embraced digital photography in the early 2000s, it was too late. By that time, other companies had taken the foothold in the digital photography space, and film development and printing seemed about as interesting as continuing to install landline phones in homes. Where was the spirit of innovation? What happened to looking forward? The executives' decisions to resist and avoid changing consumer-technology needs, and worse yet to abandon the opportunity to lead customers to the next generation of photography, actually led Kodak to file for bankruptcy in 2012.

Actions Speak Louder Than Words

Just as there are internal and external influencers for decisions, so there are for our behaviors. Think about how things like instinct, pride, fear, current needs, your environment, and future needs have influenced your behavior. Now, think about a news story or maybe a personal experience when someone's actions were not congruent with who you thought they were. Generally speaking, those are times when decisions were made that did not align with the values you though they stood for. Whenever I or my teams have dissected a crisis situation, there is usually one singular moment when a decision was made that became a tipping point for behavior that lead to the issue. However, that tipping point is generally the culmination of numerous smaller decisions that were misaligned with core values. Why? Was this because of short-term gains? Maybe there were internal corporate or external social pressures? Perhaps the person just didn't see how their decision would impact the bigger picture for the company or themselves? Could it have been a situation where the person needed to look good in front of management to keep their job? Maybe the culture had made certain nonproductive behavior by individuals acceptable?

I have had the opportunity to work with Ford over my career, and it's a company I have tremendous respect for—not only the culture, but also the people who make up this iconic American brand. Several years ago, I heard a story from a Ford executive about how Alan Mulally took over the CEO role in late 2006 and began applauding leaders for calling out mistakes—not burying them. This was prerecession, but the automotive industry was in shambles, perhaps an indicator of bigger issues to come! The story was centered on accepted behavior and, in this case, focused on product managers who were burying vehicle production issues with the intent of those issues being dealt with after the cars rolled off the production line. In some cases, this is not unusual because it costs a significant amount of money to stop the production line to fix an issue. The executive told me about regular manager meetings where they would go around the room for status check-ins on the timing of production or to discuss any vehicle issues on the production line. It apparently became common for the product managers to just go around the room and report that "everything is moving along" when in reality, it was not. The end result was that production deadlines were met, which was a key criteria for manager performance, but the accepted behavior created a poor customer experience because ultimately the car would have to be sent to the repair shop. As the story unfolds, Mulally began sitting in on these meetings. At one particular meeting, it appeared to be a business-as-usual scenario until one production manager said that they found a problem with one of the parts and that the car launch would be delayed. The exec told me that the other managers in the room were shocked and thought it was career suicide to say that in front of the CEO. What Mulally did next helped break a chain of accepted behavior. Mulally began to clap and went on to praise the manager for not only recognizing that something was wrong, but having the courage to do something about it, which ultimately created a better vehicle, which delivered a positive customer experience and ultimately helped rebuild the Ford brand and organizational culture.

Time Will Tell

There is an old saying that "time heals all wounds." I think that is a generalized statement. Also, how much time is enough time to forget or move on? Time is relative, and can move differently for each person. While other people can begin to forgive or forget questionable or negative behavior over time, our emphasis should be on what we do with that time. What you do will determine how well you rebound. If you have worked to make amends and know what went wrong and are diligent and authentic with your decisions and behavior, then, yes, such consistency, over time, will positively shape how people see you. The key words are "consistency" and "time"! Conversely, if you approach those who were hurt by your previous decisions and behavior and say you are going to make a change, but truly don't live that out, then it's easy to see why you could live another hundred years and those people would still see you as you were prior to the crisis or issue. Can you think of a situation that occurred in your life where, over time, you saw a person truly live what they said they would work on? Did it positively change the way you saw them or perhaps strengthen your relationship? Maybe that person was you?

I think back to a time in my life when I fell into a habit of canceling lunches with friends or colleagues at the last minute because "something at work had come up." I wasn't making it up—things would come up at work that I felt had to be addressed right away, and I had also rationalized it in my head because I was moving my way up the career ladder. What that decision and subsequent behavior was actually saying was that my work was more important than my friends and colleagues and the commitments I made to them. One day, I canceled a lunch with a very dear friend of mine. She said she understood, but later when I called to reschedule, she told me there would be no need because she wasn't interested in going to lunch. I thought maybe the day I offered up didn't work with her schedule, but she politely said that she was through setting up lunches only to have me cancel—that isn't what friends do over and over to each other. It was a seminal moment for me when I realized the impact of what I was doing, not just to her, but so many other people in my life. I apologized and tried to plead my case, but she held her ground. Trying to justify my thinking and actions was, quite honestly, laughable. It didn't matter because I had to own the impact of what I had done. Deep down I did know it wasn't right—I had just continued to rationalize it and believe that my friends understood and would be OK with it.

You may think canceling lunch isn't that big of a deal, but swap "lunch" for words like "meetings" or "volunteering" or "carpooling" or "grabbing coffee" or "calling back" or "repaying." While that was several years ago, from that moment, I have consistently worked to honor commitments with my friends and colleagues, and over time I have rebuilt trust with them. Am I perfect every time? Nope. But, like many of us, I am a work in progress and trying to get better every day!

Summing It Up

Consider the Reputation Equation as a grounding visual resource to help you refocus on the core of who you are, what you believe in, and how you want to be remembered. To be clear, when I say "how you want to be remembered," I'm specifically addressing your reputation in the present and future tenses, not the past tense. Both your future opportunities and legacy are dictated by the values that ground you, the decisions you make, and your subsequent behaviors. You don't have to be a mathematician to figure that one out!

Shift Points:

* Values anchor you to your personal truths—who you are and what you stand for

* Your values drive your thoughts, decisions, and your actions; you and only you are responsible for all three of them

* Recognize the power of the halo effect and that whom you associate with can have a negative or positive impact on your reputation

* Values will guide you through personal and leadership challenges

* Successful leaders see their values as their true north and are committed to them and remind themselves daily that they are not negotiable

Acceleration:

1. List the core values that guide you then put a star next to the one(s) that you find difficult or could stand to live out more consistently.

    1. _____
    2. _____
    3. _____
    4. _____
    5. _____
    6. _____
    7. _____
    8. _____

    Now write down two ways, for each difficult/inconsistent value, as to how you will incorporate those values into your daily life over the next 30 days.

    Value 1 _____
    1. _____
    2. _____

    Value 2 _____
    1. _____
    2. _____

    Value 3 _____
    1. _____
    2. _____

    Value 4 _____
    1. _____
    2. _____

2. Recall a time when you were at the crossroads of *values* and *behavior* and you had to make a difficult decision. What drove your decision? Reflecting on that now, how would you have changed your decision? Why or why not?

_____

_____

_____

_____

_____

_____

_____

3. Have you ever experienced the halo effect of association in your life? What was it?

_____

_____

_____

4. What will become your daily, visual reminder of your values?

_____

_____

_____

Chapter Five

Truth Number 4:
Move Past Your Emotions

"Being Pissed Off Isn't a Strategy"

A reputation for a thousand years may depend
upon the conduct of a single moment.
—Ernest Bramah, English Author

Sunday morning, February 18, 2001, at Daytona International Speedway began as race days typically do—traffic lining up for miles around the track; tens of thousands of fans filling the grandstands; campfires burning; the first beer of the day being cracked; vendors selling drivers T-shirts, hats, die-cast cars, and other tribal gear. Inside the bowl (the track's infield), it was business as usual for the forty-three teams getting ready to compete in NASCAR's Super Bowl—the Daytona 500. Unlike professional stick and ball sports that end their seasons with the largest and most prestigious games, NASCAR begins its season with its marquee race.

The promise and excitement of a new season filled us all. The familiar sights of those multicolored rolling billboards lining up for technical inspection and pit stalls getting set up blended with the unmistakable sounds of clanking wrenches and roaring motors, reminding us of why we love this sport.

The day started out with the brightest of possibilities for the drivers, teams, and millions of fans anxiously awaiting the green flag to wave. But that day, the checkered flag unfurled for the last time for one of the sport's most prolific competitors—Sunday afternoon, February 18, 2001, became one of the darkest days in the history of NASCAR.

Racing for five hundred miles is not only a test of endurance for the drivers, but also for their machines. With nerves of steel, these drivers deftly control their vehicles at speeds often exceeding 200 mph merely inches from the bumper of their competitors.

The field had endured 499 miles of door-to-door racing, and the final lap was shaping up to be a storybook ending for Dale Earnhardt Incorporated. Michael Waltrip was poised to win the Daytona 500. Dale Earnhardt Jr., who was still three years away from winning his first Daytona 500, was drafting off of Waltrip's rear bumper, in position to claim his best finish in this race. In third place was the legendary black No. 3 driven by a man who transcended the sport—the Intimidator, the Man in Black—Dale Earnhardt.

With less than one mile to go on the 2.5-mile superspeedway and the checkered flag about to wave, the final chapter of this fairytale became a horror story.

Waltrip and Dale Jr. began separating themselves from the field going down the backstretch, and as they drove through turns three and four, Earnhardt Sr. positioned his menacing black Chevrolet in the middle of the three racing lanes, doing his best to block the other cars vying for position. It was at that point Earnhardt Sr. got a light tap on the rear bumper by veteran driver Sterling Marlin. His car got loose, he tried to correct it, but the car quickly turned right and went straight up the turn-four banking and into the retaining wall.

The crash may not have looked very severe to the casual viewer because the No. 3 car hit the wall head on and then just skidded down the track's banking and came to rest on the grass. However, if you had been around the sport and known what to look for, you would have seen that this was a very bad wreck. Our minds conjure up images of sheet metal and parts flying off the car when we think of bad racing accidents, but it's when parts and pieces are separating from the car that the energy of the accident is dispersed away from the driver. It's accidents like Earnhardt's where the car comes to sudden stop that the driver's body absorbs much of the impact's energy. What caught my attention when watching Earnhardt's crash was the way that the hood of his car flapped in the wind like a flag.

Waltrip and Dale Jr. had the finish line in sight and finished first and second, respectively, but all eyes and attention were on the crumpled, steaming front-end of Earnhardt's machine and the fact that there was no movement inside the car. Drivers are told by NASCAR officials to put their window nets down after an accident as a sign to the safety crew that they are OK. Earnhardt's window net never moved.

Earnhardt embodied NASCAR racing at its best—he was a hard-nosed competitor, fearless, determined, passionate, loyal, and intimidating. He was a driver that fans either loved or hated. He was a force among drivers and fans. He was one of the all-time greatest drivers and personalities that ever strapped into a race car. He was gone in an instant. It was a huge personal and professional loss to all in the NASCAR garage and NASCAR nation.

Now what some outside of the sport may not know is that Earnhardt's death was the third in roughly one year due to similar injuries. Kenny Irwin and Adam Petty (grandson of Richard "the King" Petty and the shoulders upon which the future of the Petty family racing tradition had rested) both died at New Hampshire Motor Speedway within two months of each other from injuries sustained from basilar skull fractures.

Earnhardt's untimely death drew the attention of the national and international media. As fans lined up, camped out, and mourned outside the black gates of the revered Dale Earnhardt Incorporated compound, scores of media members captured b-roll and recorded interviews with his loyal followers. Beyond the fan reactions, there were also pointed questions and concerns by those who followed and participated in the sport. Is a sport that is inherently dangerous, too dangerous?

"GET ME WASHINGTON ON THE LINE!"

The late Jim Hunter, then NASCAR's communications chief, was in the inner circle that worked to find the answers and help this tight-knit community work through the frustration, anger, and grief. One of the first things Jim did was to bring in one of his old friends, a Washington heavyweight, to help navigate the situation. Jody Powell is a name that is legendary in both political and communications circles. As President Jimmy Carter's press secretary, Powell was no stranger to understanding and diffusing potentially volatile situations. Powell was called upon to work with NASCAR on how to manage the scrutiny and the reputation of the league.

I had the great opportunity to meet Jody, who passed away in September of 2009, with Jim, and they recounted a story that I believe epitomizes how to approach a crisis and is at the foundation of how we must shift our perspective on reputation management.

As Jody told me, there was a very senior meeting at NASCAR's Daytona Beach, Florida, headquarters in the wake of the Earnhardt accident. Bill France Jr., son of the founder of NASCAR, was visibly angry and quite vocal about how the media and outsiders were beating up his sport. There were scores of stories about the loss of an icon, asking how NASCAR could let this happen, about NASCAR acting too slowly on the safety front in the aftermath of the Irwin and Petty deaths, about the sport just being too dangerous. Anger and frustration are understandable emotions for a man who has spent his life nurturing and advancing a sport and who had just lost a close friend.

Jody said this tirade, understandably, went on for a while, and all in the room just listened intently to Mr. France. Jody described a room of people looking at the conference room table in front of them or with eyes fixed on the ceiling, counting tiles. When Mr. France finished speaking, silence filled the room. At that point, Jody laid it out there and said, "With all due respect, Mr. France, being pissed off is not a strategy." There are very few people in the sport who would dare say something like that to Mr. France and hope to have a job when they stopped to take a breath.

As the room went silent, the staff waited to see what his response would be. Jody said Mr. France looked him in the eye and said, "Then let's talk about what we're going do."

MOVING PAST EMOTIONS AND MAKING A PLAN

The man who had made a career out of managing messages in Washington yet again delivered the right message at the right time. Jody quickly and deftly shifted the focus from the exposed emotions and placed it on action.

That shift in perspective went from "look what's being done" to an attitude leading to empowerment—"let's talk about what we're going to do." It's a very powerful position to take, because the reality is that being pissed off is not a strategy.

So, how do we apply this approach to ourselves? Take a moment and think about the reaction we typically have when faced with a personal or brand reputation crisis. We can probably all point to a time in our lives when we found out a friend said something about us to our group of friends that was completely untrue but was taken as truth. How did you feel when you found out that you've been the target of the coworker who loves to stir the pot? The emotions you felt probably were not too different from what Mr. France was feeling—anger, frustration, fear, anxiety, confusion, to name a few. Those emotions are absolutely natural and nothing to be ashamed of. While the focus of this book is to offer proactive strategies for reputation management, the reality is that there may be a time in your life or career when you have to react to a situation. What will you do? Perhaps this has happened to you previously. What did you do? How long did you linger on your feelings? Did you have a plan of what to do next, or did you just wing it?

What's done next is usually what separates those who successfully save their reputations from those who don't—that next step is critical.

I typically look at three things when determining how someone will emerge from this type of situation: 1. How long do they linger on their emotions? 2. How soon do they get to the action-based plan? 3. How good is the plan? Yes, believe it or not, we all need a plan.

How Long Do They Linger on Their Emotions?

I clearly remember Mrs. Martinez, my high school sociology teacher, talking about the roles of emotions in society. Her headline for this lesson was simple: emotions are neither good nor bad, they just are. It's healthy to feel and embrace them when in an emotional situation, which an attack on your reputation can be. However, when faced with a crisis, there is a point in time when you have to move your focus beyond *what's been done* to *what you will do*. Time is always a limited resource when you are in the middle of a crisis.

Domino's Pizza faced an epic crisis situation in 2009 when two employees posted a video on YouTube of them doing very unsanitary things to pizza toppings before placing them on the pizza. Views of the video rose increasing rapidly, and the brand needed to respond quickly.

Tim McIntyre, the vice president of communications for Domino's Pizza reflected on the experience in an article in the Public Relations Society of America's *The Strategist* magazine.

"My first reaction when I saw it was anger," McIntyre said. "I was angry because I love this place, I love this brand, I love the franchisees that I work with. And I took it personally—that it was a personal affront to everything that I've come to know about this company in the past twenty-four years. But my immediate reaction was to send the link to a couple of core people—our social media people, our head of security, senior management—to say, 'This has been posted, we need to do something about it. Let's begin.' There were a few of us on this immediate response team, and we channeled anger into action."

The sooner you can embrace, digest, and release your emotions around a specific situation, the sooner you will be able to focus your energy on the critical next steps.

Conversely, there is an epic story about Amy's Baking Company that was featured on Chef Gordon Ramsay's *Kitchen Nightmares* television show. The show features restaurants in distress, and the renowned chef will work with the owners to identify the issues with the ultimate intent of helping them succeed. In the case of Amy's Baking Company, it was the first time in the show's history where Ramsay had to walk away from an assignment. In some instances, the owners would yell at and throw customers out of the restaurant if they complained about the food. As well, there were allegations that they stole employee's tips.

After the show aired, the restaurant did not come off in a positive light—as you can imagine. Yelp and Facebook reviews began pouring in with negative comments from customers. Instead of dealing with the negativity and addressing the issues, the owners decided to take to social media with their own, emotionally charged feedback.

Facebook posts, such as these all capitalized ones have made their way around the Internet:

"I AM NOT STUPID ALL OF YOU ARE. YOU JUST DO NOT KNOW GOOD FOOD."

"WE ARE NOT FREAKING OUT. PISS OFF ALL OF YOU. BRING IT. WE WILL FIGHT BACK."

The show aired in May of 2013, and Amy's Baking Company reportedly closed its doors in September of 2015.

Think back to how Mr. France handled the situation when reflecting on your own feelings, and then get moving!

HOW SOON DO THEY GET TO THE ACTION-BASED PLAN?

There was a legendary NASCAR engine builder named Smokey Yunick who used to say, "Speed costs money. How fast do you want to go?"

The speed at which you recognize and respond to a reputation attack can cost you more than money. Social media's expansive and responsive nature requires our immediate attention when it comes to managing reputations.

From a corporate perspective, brand managers are dealing with more empowered and connected consumers. What had historically been a monologue from a brand to a consumer has now become a dialogue between consumers, with brands trying to elbow their way into the conversation. Consider that nearly 80 percent of online consumers consider reviews extremely influential when making purchasing decisions.

It was acceptable a decade ago to respond to and publicly address a crisis situation within forty-eight hours of news breaking. Now, if a company doesn't respond in some way to negative news within a few hours of news coverage or social media posts, many view this as a failed effort to manage a crisis. That is because the court of public opinion will not only deliver its verdict, independent of a company's evidence or defense, but those citizen journalists will also begin to circulate their own opinions to their social networks.

Personal reputation attacks are no different. Consider that it's your reputation that speaks for you when you aren't there to speak for yourself. Your personal reputation is what opens the doors of opportunity or padlocks shut the very same door.

A Jobvite Social Recruiting Survey found that 92 percent of employers use or plan to use social media networks for recruiting. Consider your social media footprints as digital extensions of your analog reputation. Why is it important to ensure you have cultivated a strong and positive social presence? According to a CareerBuilder survey, 34 percent of hiring managers found information about a candidate through social media channels that caused them *not* to hire that individual. Some of those reasons were the posting of inappropriate material or bad-mouthing current or previous employers. The lesson here is to think before you hit "post."

On the flip side, 29 percent of those hiring managers actually found something via social outlets that caused them to move forward and *hire* the candidate. These gatekeepers found strong references, examples of creativity and well-rounded interests as well as great communications skills.

While Smokey was talking about creating horsepower for stock cars, today's social media outlets are the horsepower for harnessing the power of your reputation. Waiting too long to put your plan into action could cost you money, opportunities, and even a second chance!

How Good Is the Plan?

There's an old saying that we'd use in PR when it came to crisis management, and it goes like this, "If you fail to plan, you plan to fail."

Crisis plans are not exclusively for corporations, which typically have corporate communications teams that have crisis management plans at the ready. You may own a small- to mid-sized business. Perhaps you are an entrepreneur or maybe you own an insurance agency or a franchise? Maybe you are looking for a new job or want that promotion? Crisis is never a question of "if," it's always a matter of "when." So, the real question is, "Are you prepared?"

Taking a proactive approach to managing your reputation is one of the best ways to get through any crisis. What does that mean? The best defense is a strong offense.

So, how does that work? One way is to regularly carve out time during an afternoon or evening, maybe a Friday or a Sunday, and reflect on the week in your life and assess your actions. Have you followed through on the commitments you've made? How have you worked with and treated colleagues, friends, or family? How were you living your values? These are just a few example questions you can ask yourself to see how you are either managing or mismanaging your reputation on a daily basis.

If the time does come when you need to put a plan into action, it's critical to have a checklist that you can reference and act on. You must first recognize what was at the epicenter of the situation, beyond the "who," "why," and "how" questions. Then the plan must outline who has been impacted and how you plan to address these people. It should also have a timeline with measurable steps and outcomes. And most importantly, there has to be a commitment for future actions to avoid walking down the same broken road, time after time. Another component that is critical in our socially connected world is to identify the resources (i.e., people) who can help you work through your situation and tell your side of the story.

Use the following questions as a foundation of your plan checklist:

Reflection

- Have you honestly identified the root cause of the issue?

- How will you address the root cause of the issue?

- Is what is being said about you true?

- Where have you built up "credits" among your network and is this the time to "cash" some of them in?

- Are your words consistent with your beliefs?

- Are you committed to walking the walk after you've talked the talk?

Action

- What will you do to change the situation (short term and long term)?

- What will you say and have you communicated it with the right people?

- When will you begin this plan?

- When will you complete it?

- What will be different when you are done?

- How will you measure the difference?

- How will you keep yourself accountable to ensure you don't make the same mistake twice?

"SAYS WHO?"

I developed a versatile and proactive reputation management resource when I was at Sprint Nextel that I called our "Says Who?" sheet. As the Sprint Nextel merger began to pick up momentum, it got fans, industry, and media members wondering what was going to happen during and after the corporate integration. You see, Sprint had been in the sport for many years and actually sponsored Adam Petty as well as his father, Kyle. So, there were questions about Sprint's continued interest in NASCAR. There were questions about budget restrictions and reductions, which can translate into questioning a sponsor's commitment to the sport—would this post-merger company continue to live up to its promise? Or would it just maintain the status quo? There were questions surrounding key executives who had been the stewards of the sponsorship leaving. What about new technology investments and product launches? You name it, we were being asked. The pace at which these daily questions were asked sometimes felt like interrogations by both media and fans.

We actually had great answers about the ongoing technical support and financial horsepower that Sprint would deliver post-merger. So, I started a list of the questions we were regularly being asked and listed every answer and example of how we were still committed to the NASCAR platform. Then, with my communications team, we came up with other questions that might be asked and specific answers and examples for those, too. This was essentially our way of proactively answering the questions with "Really? Not committed to the NASCAR partnership? Says who? Because here's what we have going on . . ."

This proactive approach helped us educate both our media

partners and industry constituents about what was happening during the merger and the forward-looking work that was being planned as well as funded. Often, we were getting positive stories written about the ongoing efforts during the merger. Sometimes, the payout was just an appreciative journalist who said, "Thanks for the update." and wrote nothing—which, many communications professionals can attest, can be just as valuable as a front-page headline!

Many times reputation attacks catch people and brands off guard and therefore they aren't prepared to deal with them appropriately. Again, while each reputation attack is invariably unique, there are vulnerabilities that you can identify. As the steward of your personal brand, you can better prepare your "Says Who?" sheet by understanding your potential areas of weakness. Keep in mind that this tool can also become a plan for you or your company. If you find that you do not have positive or powerful answers when someone challenges you, this resource will identify the gaps and show you where and what you need to be doing. Invest some time in this exercise and you'll be more prepared and better directed as a result.

SHIFT POINTS:

- Quickly move from an emotional/victim "why me?" state of reflection to a "what am I going to do?" empowered/leader mindset

- Once you hit "post," you have created a digital footprint that can either help or hurt your reputation and future opportunities

- There is no room to be reactive as a leader; actions must be proactive

- Leaders anticipate negative scenarios and are prepared to respond accordingly

Acceleration:

1. On a scale of 1–5 (1 being many hours and 5 being minutes) how long do you focus on your emotions before determining your action?

1   2   3   4   5

2. Recall the last three proactive decisions/actions you have made. How did it turn out? Now, finish this sentence . . .

   "I believe it's important to move from a victim's mentality to an empowered state because . . ."

   _____

   _____

   _____

3. List 5 strategies you can use to ensure your digital footprint truly reflects you:

   Digital Footprint Strategy 1

   _____

   _____

   Digital Footprint Strategy 2

   _____

   _____

   Digital Footprint Strategy 3

   _____

   _____

DIGITAL FOOTPRINT STRATEGY 4

DIGITAL FOOTPRINT STRATEGY 5

---

4. Reflect and write down the three areas in your life or business where you feel most vulnerable to a reputation attack. Now, write down your "Says Who?" statements for each of those areas. You may find that you have some work to do to fill in those statements. That's OK, write down what statement you would need in order to become less vulnerable and get to work on it!

REPUTATION VULNERABILITY 1

"SAYS WHO?" 1

REPUTATION VULNERABILITY 2

"SAYS WHO?"

Reputation Vulnerability 3

_____

_____

"Says Who?"

_____

_____

Chapter Six

TRUTH NUMBER 5:
VISUALIZE YOUR PERSONAL INSTANT REPLAY
Emotions in High Gear Can Drive Reputation Bankruptcy

It takes twenty years to build a reputation and five minutes to ruin it. If you think about that, you'll do things differently.
—*Warren Buffett, Financier*

"EMOTIONAL SOUVENIRS" ARE THOSE EXPERIENCES SPORTS FANS never outgrow. When I worked at The Marketing Arm, a global sports, entertainment, and consumer-promotions agency, we designed all of our work around the state of emotion in an effort to create what we called emotional souvenirs—experiences that forge relationships, the money-can't-buy moments that last a lifetime. These are the experiences that create memories that outlast the commemorative team cup that fades after a few years of dishwashing, your favorite player's jersey that you outgrow, or the wall poster that gets lost during a move.

Emotion is the signature of sport and what we have come to love about athletes and how they play the game.

Race car drivers are an ultracompetitive group. It's a sport where the playing field moves in only one direction and the competitors are worried about more than one opponent. If you think about it, it's one of the few sports that doesn't offer a 50/50 chance of winning. Which leads us back to why these drivers are so competitive and can be very emotional—and by emotional I mean they can be short-fused when their day ends due to another driver's mistake.

We typically see their competitive passion come to life on TV during postwreck interviews—where the reporter and camera crew walk up to the driver standing by their damaged car and ask the obvious question, "What happened out there?"

Motorsports media coverage truly captures real-time emotion. There is no other sport where cameras and microphones are shoved in an athlete's face immediately after something has happened to them on the field. What do you think Shaquille O'Neal would say, back when he was playing, if a microphone was put in his face on the sideline during the game after missing free throw after free throw? It just doesn't happen.

This type of media access and real-time reporting puts a spotlight on the human aspect that has made motorsports so popular over the years—the question of what is going to come out of the driver's mouth after an accident or when another driver hits their car—the sheer frustration, anger, sarcasm, humor, or honesty is what keeps fans talking, posting, and commenting both during the race and for days to come.

RACE CARS AND ROCKETS

My first opportunity to work in this field came from Tom Cotter, an innovator and pioneer in motorsports public relations. His creativity, curiosity, work ethic, strong network of contacts, and passion shaped my view of not only what a career in this industry could be but the power of a strong reputation. Early in my career at Cotter Group, which was a leading motorsports agency, I oversaw the public relations for Western Auto's motorsports efforts in both NASCAR and NHRA drag racing.

Professional drag racing is one of the most extreme forms of motorsports. Watching race cars with six thousand horsepower reach speeds of more than 300 mph in less than a quarter of a mile is a sight and sound that isn't soon forgotten. An interesting comparison to illustrate the sheer power of these four-wheeled rockets is that each cylinder in a NHRA Top Fuel car's engine has the same amount of horsepower as one NASCAR Cup Series stock car engine. Another interesting fact is that a Top Fuel driver will experience more g-forces when the car launches from the starting line than a NASA astronaut does when a space shuttle leaves the launch pad.

The Funny Car, which is a different competitive NHRA class, produces similar horsepower to a Top Fuel dragster but look distinctively different. While they both have the large rear tires, Funny Cars bodies lift up so the driver can crawl into the seat, while there is no outer body shell for a Top Fuel dragster.

Now, one of the Funny Car drivers I worked with was long-time wheelman Al Hoffman. Al had the reputation in the sport for his tenacious attitude toward competitors as well as his gruff and intimidating personality. And the speed of his Funny Car was only matched by the speed of his quick wit!

He would do and say things that many of us would typically just keep in our heads. Have you been around people like this? There was really no filter for Al, and he was unapologetic about it. He didn't live in a politically correct world. He didn't live in a world with the luxury of time to talk and work things out. In his world, success or failure was a three-and-a-half second burst of speed toward the finish line. Never looking back, always looking forward. No time to think. Instinct and action rule the day. Sometimes those actions would just leave us standing there sucking air through our gaping mouths in disbelief.

Kitchen Island vs. Refrigerator

We had an affectionate nickname for Al among our agency team. We called him "Chainsaw."

As Al told the story, he was nearing the completion of a kitchen remodel in his home when he observed the construction crew standing beside the new kitchen island that was installed. It was obvious to Al that they were trying to figure something out. For a man whose life was spent going as fast as he could, he couldn't stand when things (and people) were going slow.

He eventually went into the kitchen, and as he told us, he asked what was happening—or, in this case, what was *not* happening?

Apparently, there had been a miscalculation when the crew measured the distance between the new island and how much space they needed to get the new, larger refrigerator in the house and installed. Al said they were just wasting time trying to figure out how to get the refrigerator past the island and were throwing out ideas on how they could bring it in without ruining the island.

Al said he had had enough of talking and he would be back to take care of the situation. He returned a few minutes later with a chainsaw, fired it up, and cut the island in half as the crew stood there completely dumbfounded. Once the sawdust settled and the chainsaw went silent after spitting wood chips around the kitchen, Al told them to get the refrigerator in and take care of the island—issue resolved, Chainsaw style!

Speed not Feed

Now, there are other times when you have to assess your environment and consider that thoughts should just stay as that—thoughts.

Race track promoters often hold fan festivals when the race comes to town. It's a great way to get local media attention for the upcoming event, and it gives fans a chance to meet their favorite drivers and get memorabilia signed and pictures with their heroes.

At one particular NHRA fan event, around one thousand fans lined up to meet the various drivers, have their pictures taken with them, and have driver hero cards, T-shirts, or die-cast cars signed. The event was running smoothly, the drivers and fans were all having a great time.

About midway through the event, a husband and wife stepped up to Al's table for an autograph. Now, the husband was about 6' 2" and as wide as a No. 2 pencil. His wife was not. She was around 5' 5" and much heavier than her husband.

As Al was signing one of his hero cards, the husband wanted to make some small talk and asked him, "So, Al, do you think she'll go 325 this weekend?" He was referring to the top speed of Al's Funny Car. And, Al, who never missed a one-liner, looked up from the table, surveyed the couple, and without skipping a beat said, "Buddy, she'll go 350 if you keep feeding her." And he went right back to signing the hero card.

It was literally one of those "did that just happen?" moments. The husband nervously laughed, the wife's jaw dropped.

The wife began to say a few words when her husband took her arm and walked away. Al looked up, shrugged his shoulders and said, "Well, he asked."

How Much Rope Would You Like?

The stories above took place years before social media was developed—it's a completely different world now! Reputation management has had to change because one-liners live on in a new way.

Social media channels have not only become great avenues of promotion and connection, but for those in the public eye, it's also become a living tightrope.

Americus Reed, a professor of marketing at Wharton, said in a February 2013 article titled "The Hazards of Celebrity Endorsements in the Age of Twitter" that social media gives celebrities "more rope with which to hang themselves. It has leveled the playing field by which people can spread information—everyone with a cell phone has the potential to be a journalist. And the story can be sustained and live on for a much longer time."

Think about the posts or stories we read about fans' experiences with or around celebrities spread like wildfire on Twitter. How about the tweet about Justin Bieber using a restaurant's kitchen floor mop bucket as a urinal? What about Clint Eastwood's empty-chair monologue at the 2012 Republican National Convention? Who could forget Charlie Sheen and his "tiger blood" rant?

How many of those "restaurant receipt" news stories have we seen, where employees add an unflattering or sexist comment to a receipt meant only for colleagues to see, but it ends up in the customer's hands and then ultimately is seen by thousands of people online? These generally lead to a public apology by the company and often the dismissal of the employee. Why? Because someone didn't think.

So here's the simple lesson and thought that many don't realize: Our reputations are the sum of our consistent daily decisions over time. Our reputations are the accumulation of what we say or don't say, what we do or don't do. More importantly, our reputations are not formed in perfect scenarios where people make decisions in an objective manner. People around us, especially those who connect with us mainly through social channels, see snapshots of who we are, which makes it critical that they experience consistency in those connection points. Based on how people know and interact with us—social media followers versus live, daily experiences—our reputations can look like mosaics rather than crisp images because in many instances people are just seeing small glimpses of our actions and lives.

THE INTERNET NEVER FORGETS

The interesting thing about social networking is that we often take a very carefree attitude about what we say and share because we are among friends, right? And usually we are posting what looks like our living highlight reel, the great things we are doing or places we are going with our family and friends. Rarely do we see our blooper reel being posted—the mistakes we make, the imperfections we have, sometimes our in-the-moment thoughts that shouldn't be posted. And, of course we have seen examples of people posting negative comments about their bosses and soon after getting fired. Or, how about the video that a bystander captures that gets posted and incriminates other people?

An amazing example of viral video is when NASCAR driver Kurt Busch fell out of the 2011 season-ending race at Homestead-Miami Speedway due to a transmission failure. Busch already had a reputation among the media as often times being unpredictable when it comes to interviews.

In this case, Busch was waiting to be interviewed by ESPN's Dr. Jerry Punch, a very well-respected person and journalist within the sports community. While Busch and Punch were waiting to go live with the interview, a fan was standing near them, capturing the conversation. Busch was clearly frustrated to have to wait for the live interview and was getting more agitated by some of Punch's comments and questions as they stood there in the garage area. The fan captured Busch cursing at Punch and the camera crew while they waited for the signal that they were live. It ended in a way that surprised many in the industry—Punch had heard enough and ended the interview before it even started. He can be seen speaking into the microphone to the control booth and saying, "You know what? Nevermind, nevermind." And he walks away from Busch.

Busch went on to later publicly apologize for his actions and had sought out support for how to better manage his frustration and attitude. Many of us in the industry have seen a very different Kurt Busch over the past few years in his interviews and how he continues to handle his behavior and control his emotions.

Now, that exchange would never have been seen if it weren't for a video that went viral. We have to remember that what we say and share can easily be shared with a global audience.

While we focus on how our actions and behavior influences our reputations, we must also be mindful that what may be forgotten among friends over time will never be erased from the Internet.

The *New York Times* ran an article titled "The Web Means the End of Forgetting" that dug into the implications of the digital Wild West that has unlimited information, unlimited sharing, and unlimited searching capabilities. Contributing writer and George Washington University law professor Jeffrey Rosen addressed the challenge that we now face:

> How best to live our lives in a world where the Internet records everything and forgets nothing—where every online photo, status update, Twitter post and blog entry by and about us can be stored forever. With web sites like LOL Facebook Moments, which collects and shares embarrassing personal revelations from Facebook users, ill-advised photos and online chatter are coming back to haunt people months or years after the fact.

As a result, an entire industry has emerged in the search engine optimization field to help people clean up their social networking house. If you do a quick Google search for "reputation management services" you'll be able to scroll through more than 10.7 million results. HubSpot released the results of a survey it conducted among SEO agencies to better understand the range of monthly retainer service fees. The survey found that nearly 50 percent of SEO agencies charge between $1,000 and $5,000 per month for their services—it's quite an industry.

These services can certainly provide value, but the fact remains that the online content you don't want family, friends, or current or prospective employers to see is still available for review—it's only buried deeper on the search pages. This SEO strategy is largely built upon the predictable behavior that 91 percent of people will not click 'next' and go to the second page of a Google results page.

Recruiters and employers are essentially trying to piece together digital mosaics of candidates, and they do so by searching for "pieces" of their social presence—both past and present. But what happens if the pieces don't create a flattering image? The reality may be that the candidate pieced together through employment recruiters' social media filtering does not truly reflect the essence or character of the applicant. That would be unfortunate, but may not matter because as the old saying goes, "perception is reality."

Eric Schmidt, chairman of Google, expressed a highly contested opinion in a *Wall Street Journal* interview that illustrated a possible, yet extreme, degree of action in order for people to escape a tarnished digital image.

"Every young person one day will be entitled automatically to change his or her name on reaching adulthood in order to disown the youthful hijinks stored on their friends' social media sites."

Schmidt goes on to say, "I don't believe society understands what happens when everything is available, knowable and recorded by everyone all the time."

As a society, we truly do not understand the personal and professional implications or the socio-evolutions that will come as a result of social hyperconnectivity.

Some experts believe that with ever-evolving data-mining and tracking software, digital social profiling will become the norm. What will that create? We now see this with online star reviews, which are generated through consumer interactions and experiences with you or people representing your company. But how about a personal reputation score? Think of these reputation scores like our current credit score system where lenders gauge a person's viability for borrowing money and paying it back. These scores would reflect the opinions of others on their experiences and interactions with you to quantify or grade, for example, a person's dependability, work ethic, trustworthiness, or relationship potential.

Could You Declare Reputation Bankruptcy?

This is another example of the Reputation Economy's impact.

In 2014, there were nearly 910,000 nonbusiness (meaning personal) bankruptcy filings in the United States. Now, the fact that these people had to declare bankruptcy could be due to a number of reasons—perhaps it was just poor financial decisions? Maybe it was because of a chain of events such as the company they worked for going out of business and they lost their job and went into debt to pay the bills? Or, the person may just be over their head financially and believe that bankruptcy is the only option to get out and move on?

There's a parallel in those scenarios and decisions to our personal reputations and the impact it has on our ability to earn more or have better future opportunities presented to us.

Some people simply do not understand or appreciate the value of reputations. Others associate themselves with less reputable people or organizations, which brings down their own reputations—always remember the halo effect of association. Still others have consistently acted in a way that has irreparably ruined their reputations with little hope of improvement.

Jonathan Zittrain, author and cofounder and codirector of the Berkman Klein Center for Internet and Society at Harvard University, has put forth another option for consideration in this Reputation Economy where we often gauge a person's (or our own) social value or worth by the "like," "favorite," "share," or "retweet" buttons—what if we were able to declare Reputation Bankruptcy? What if your digital reputation would reset after a certain period of time? This idea certainly shines a light on the alignment between our real-life interactions with people and the interactions we have online. Zittrain explains in an NPR Marketplace Tech Report radio interview with John Moe how this could work, similar to how our personal financial credit scores exist.

"As we see a world in which more and more, this vector being created digitally for you that various intermediaries are recommending you to others, or maybe not recommending you to others," Zittrain begins. "You get to the question of if I want to curate that, if I want to have some say in how I'm seen other than having hidden algorithms determine what my worth is to other people, how can I do that?

"My hope would be to see a world in which the intermediaries, themselves, have been persuaded to not just only answer to themselves on how they rate people and rank them, but to understand that there should be some elements of fairness in there. So one element of fairness that might be easy to implement is after a while bad stuff, at least, and maybe good stuff, too, should expire. This is America, there are second acts, you can reinvent yourself and you don't want to have one misstep hurt you forever.

"So there ought to be ways in which the system can naturally, either in a rolling basis fade out or appropriately discount stuff that happened a long time ago, or even allow the kind of one-time pulling of a lever so that you can discharge your old or growing reputation and get another chance."

Asking for Forgiveness

Remember former New York governor Eliot Spitzer? As you may recall, Spitzer, whose term lasted a mere fifteen months, was an ardent crusader against crime, especially prostitution. As Steve Nelson, writer for U.S. News & World Report, wrote, "one of his notable achievements was enacting a law in 2007 that extended the sanction for patronizing prostitutes from three months to one year in jail."

However, after Spitzer's bank reported irregular transactions to the Treasury Department's Financial Crimes Enforcement Network, a financial investigation began. The IRS Criminal Investigation Division soon got involved because there was concern that Spitzer may have been being extorted or perhaps had his identity stolen.

He was soon identified as "Client 9," a long-standing patron of an elite escort service. It didn't take long before Spitzer was standing before cameras resigning from public office with his wife Silda at his side.

While out of office, Spitzer tried his hand at TV commentating and writing for various publications. In July of 2013, he thought it was time to come back and announced that he would be running for public office again—this time for comptroller of New York City.

He summed up his hopes of redemption in an interview with the *New York Times*—"I'm hopeful there will be forgiveness, I am asking for it."

New York is a tough city in which to find forgiveness, and Spitzer did not win the bid for the seat that could have signaled his public and political redemption.

Beyond the professional loss, Spitzer and his wife of more than two decades finalized their divorce in April of 2014 with a

$7.5 million lump-sum payment to Silda along with their Fifth Avenue apartment and a new car every five years.

Do you recall the name Justine Sacco? You may remember her tweet just prior to boarding a flight to Africa that read, "Going to Africa. Hope I don't get AIDs. Just kidding. I'm white!" Sacco, who at the time of the tweet was the senior director of corporate communications at IAC, boarded her flight from Heathrow, England, to Cape Town, South Africa and thought nothing more of her comment. When she turned her phone on after the eleven-hour flight, she was bombarded with messages, texts, and voice mails. One message, according to a story in the Feb. 12, 2015, issue of the *New York Times Magazine*, was from a friend Sacco hadn't heard from since high school, which read, "I'm so sorry to see what's happening." A baffled Sacco answered her phone to hear her best friend's voice saying, "You're the number one worldwide trend on Twitter right now." This was followed by her seeing a tweet from her employer that read, "This is an outrageous, offensive comment. Employee in question currently unreachable on an intl flight." She was released from her job soon after.

You may not remember who Alicia Lynch is, but perhaps you heard the story of her Halloween costume that reportedly also got her fired. Lynch didn't think through the potential impact of dressing up as a Boston Marathon runner hurt in the 2013 bombing attack that killed five people and injured more than 180. Six months after the attack, she went to a work Halloween party dressed in running gear with fake blood smudged on her face, legs, and arms—and then posted a picture on Twitter. She later received a comment from a victim of the bombing saying, "You should be ashamed, my mother lost both her legs and I almost died." Lynch did lose her job and her family got pulled into the social media frenzy that resounded for several months. In an interview with BuzzFeed, she said, "My family didn't know what I was doing. And they are all getting dragged into this for something I did. I made a mistake. I just have to learn from it. I'm not a terrible person."

VISUALIZE YOUR INSTANT REPLAY

What happens when an instant replay is shown during any sporting event? Does it show the play in question in slow motion? Of course. That is usually done to slow down something that has happened very quickly to get a clearer picture of the play. But, the instant replay also allows the referees to see the play from multiple vantage points in order to see what happened because, as we all know, things look differently from different perspectives. What if we incorporated our own instant replay strategy into our decision-making process? What if we all took a few moments to think through how an action or social media post would look from multiple perspectives in our lives? Perhaps something might seem funny in your social life, but be completely offensive in your work life. Would it be seen as insensitive? Would it be appropriate? Only you can answer those questions, but I can't help but wonder how might their lives and experiences have been different if Eliot, Justine, and Alicia had thought about visualizing their own instant replay.

Zittrain is right; this is America, we can evolve, change, and reinvent ourselves. We can learn from our mistakes. We can ask for forgiveness. So, what does it take to do that? Do you need a high-profile platform to begin a mea culpa, like celebrities, athletes or entertainers have? Can you tap into a legion of adoring fans who will come to your defense on social channels? What about having the financial resources to sustain you if you are unhireable for a while?

The answers to those questions are not easy, even for celebrities, athletes, and politicians who have those resources and more, which makes second chances more attainable. We mere mortals also have the same ability to begin a reputation makeover, but we must take stock in the resources we have and things we can control.

We live in a world where we try to control all of the areas in our lives, which tends to be an exercise in frustration as well as, at times, futility. That is because, in many cases, there are so any variables in play that it would require exquisite gamesmanship to manipulate and then align so many external elements in your favor on a consistent, day-to-day basis.

In my estimation, there is really only one variable that we can control that will change any outcome in any situation. Our actions. But not just actions, consistent actions. Let me give you two simple and age-old words that will be the best value for your dollar—just think. In our current world of instant news, instant information, instant contact, and instant sharing, resist the urge to jump into instant action—think about what you are about to say, do, post, or share.

Getting back to the example of emotions of race car drivers that I started off this chapter with, we now often see motorsports TV reporters using the instant replay to great effect during races. Now, instead of the pit road reporter blindly asking the driver, "What happened out there?" after an accident, they are often armed with a small TV monitor where they show the driver the instant replay so they can see the situation from a different perspective. More often than not, the driver's comments are objective about what just happened or even surprised that they were the last link in a chain of events starting several cars ahead of them. The bottom line is that the ability to see the instant replay gives them perspective and, most importantly, gives them pause to see the situation, collect their thoughts, and decide how to act.

We should all consider using this personal instant replay truth.

The reality is that we can't see into the future or forecast how a real-time situation will ultimately play out. However, taking the time to institute your instant replay of what could happen is something that can proactively be done to help you think through your options, your choices, and ultimately your actions, which, over time, will shape your reputation.

Shift Points:

- Leaders must stop, think, and forecast how their actions could play out and be seen from multiple perspectives

- A leader or person of influence is never off the clock or off duty; people place higher expectations on leaders

- Reputations are often not seen objectively; social media can make them subjective with a mosaic perspective rather than a mirror image of who you truly are

- Consistent actions must align with your core values in order to reflect your authentic self

Acceleration:

1. Reflect and write about a decision you made where using your Instant Replay could have changed the outcome for the better.

    _____

    _____

    _____

    _____

2. What decision are you now wrestling with where you can use your own Instant Replay? How will this strategy help you?

    _____

    _____

    _____

    _____

3. List five people in your life whom you admire for a certain consistent behavior. Then, next to their name, write that behavior. Finally, put a star next to the behavior you want to emulate. How will these behaviors benefit you or your business?

    Person 1 _____
    Person 2 _____
    Person 3 _____
    Person 4 _____
    Person 5 _____

    ### Behavior Benefit

    _____

    _____

    _____

4. What are three actions you will take over the next seven days to ensure that your family, friends, colleagues or customers see your authentic self?

    AUTHENTIC ACTION 1

    _____

    _____

    _____

    AUTHENTIC ACTION 2

    _____

    _____

    _____

    AUTHENTIC ACTION 3

    _____

    _____

    _____

Chapter Seven

GETTING CAUGHT UP IN THE REPUTATION MARBLES

Close Calls, Wrecks, and Redemption

Your brand name is only as good as your reputation.
—*Sir Richard Branson, Entrepreneur & Philanthropist*

THERE'S A PHRASE IN NASCAR RACING—"getting caught up in the marbles"—and it's usually used at racetracks such as Bristol Motor Speedway, Martinsville Speedway, or Richmond International Raceway. These are short tracks that are equal to or less than one mile in length, but don't let that fool you into thinking the racing is any less intense. The drivers are still racing at speeds over 100 mph and experiencing significant g-forces every single lap of the 400- to 500-mile race.

Over the course of the race, as you can imagine or may have seen, little pieces of rubber from Goodyear racing tires begin to wear off and often gather up near the racetrack's retaining wall and can be balled up, resembling a marble. The buildup of this rubber can look like a black ring at the base of the retaining wall at some tracks, and drivers do their best to steer clear of the marbles when possible. It's a natural occurrence in racing, and there's nothing particularly special about it. The simple reason it causes problems is that when a driver does get caught up in the marbles, the car's tires lose grip with the racetrack and can begin to slide. The driver can lose control and hit the wall. It doesn't matter if they have the best car in the field, getting caught up in the marbles can end their day and send them to pit road for repairs thus losing critical on-track position. In some cases the driver can lose control but scrape the wall, save the car, and stay in the race.

We've all heard that life is a race and there are many philosophical ideas to support or negate the truths behind being in the corporate "rat race" or in a race to "keep up with the Joneses." Regardless of your belief or place in either theory, we do have to recognize and be mindful of not getting caught up in the marbles in our own lives. These are the situations we may put ourselves in that we know are not right for us—maybe we've rationalized ourselves to this place? Or, perhaps the actions and decisions we make consistently over time could come back in a negative way—could they be from the blind spots in our lives? To make it easy, you could call these areas Reputation Marbles—the areas that, if you end up in, would cause damage to the reputation you've worked to build.

So, what happens when you find yourself there? Is that it? Is that the end? Just suck it up and *hope* that it all goes away and people will just forget?

Just as Jody Powell told Bill France Jr. that "being pissed off is not a strategy," I often tell the people on my teams, "hope is not a plan"—just hoping that your reputation can be restored after a crisis situation is naïve.

The Social Machine Never Sleeps

The comeback. Redemption. The underdog. Vindication.

We are a society that looks to and accepts second chances. We recognize that people are, indeed, human and make mistakes. But, as we know, even the smallest slipup can have significant implications because of social media's and word of mouth's immediate and global reach. And, when the action, sound bite, picture, or video begins to circulate and gain viral momentum, watch out. There's a digital mob mentality where people are sharing, forwarding, and retweeting their comments and opinions, serving up sentences that have significant implications in the court of public opinion.

One of the earliest examples of this is veteran radio DJ Don Imus. Imus, who was an icon in terrestrial radio for more than three decades, was one of the first radio DJs to bring his show to a live morning television broadcast. While his radio show was broadcast by CBS radio, MSNBC picked up the *Imus in the Morning* program and gave viewers a rarely seen view of how a live radio show came to life. It was a trailblazing time in cable news media.

The fuse was lit one morning in April, when Imus made an off-handed comment about the Rutgers women's basketball team. Do you remember this? He was talking sports when he mentioned that he had watched the Rutgers-Tennessee game the night before and said, "That's some rough girls from Rutgers. Man, they got tattoos, and . . . that's some nappy-headed hos there."

Imus, more than likely, didn't give it significant thought. He had made a career as one of the first "shock jocks" and had built an "I'll-say-what-I-want-to-say" reputation. However, he more than likely was also not aware of the seismic shift of public interaction and the scale, immediacy, and power of their voices being heard.

This was in 2007 and twenty-four-hour news channels were searching for content, case in point being the Imus radio show having video cameras installed in the studio to put faces to the voices. Forum message boards were extremely popular at this time, and blogging was also gaining traction, momentum, and credibility as the way for journalists and nonjournalists to dispense and express views and opinions on any subject of interest. Keep in mind that Twitter was only eleven months old and Facebook just three years old—both very much in the infancy of social adoption.

The Imus incident fueled not just traditional media ire, but also ignited cries for justice among bloggers. It became one of the first examples of how one comment in this new world of digital megaphones, which gave birth to online citizen journalists, could shatter a reputation. The rules of engagement had indeed changed.

"Today, with bloggers, all-news networks and preachers looking for sermons, Imus was a shock jock in a new era of instant judgment. He failed the test," said Tom McPhail, communications professor, University of Missouri—St. Louis.

The Rutgers comment was made on April 7. The outpouring of negative comments across the blogosphere as well as public statements by civil leaders and other news "celebrities" who were aggressively trying to build their own brands prompted numerous corporate sponsors of the show to make public statements separating themselves from Imus. By April 12, MSNBC executives were feeling the backlash and, more importantly, recognizing the impact of the reputation halo that surrounded the television network and host. The network released a statement saying that it would no longer be televising the Imus show. CBS radio, which was the mothership of his radio show, followed suit the next day.

Paul Farhi's lead in his April 13 Washington Post story titled "Don Imus Is Fired by CBS Radio" said it all: "Bowing to a national outcry and internal protest, CBS Radio said yesterday it would end Don Imus's morning program 'immediately,' possibly bringing the broadcaster's four-decade career to a swift and ignominious end."

Another example of how the court of public opinion can rule is a woman who had an ongoing joke with her friend about taking pictures of themselves disobeying signs, such as smoking by a "No Smoking" sign or parking in front of a "No Parking" sign. Lindsey Stone was visiting Arlington National Cemetery and saw a sign at the Tomb of the Unknowns. The sign read, "Silence and Respect." Stone had her picture taken as she posed with her mouth open as if she were screaming and gave the camera the middle finger. She then posted it to Facebook, but without the context of the joke, many thought she was making fun of the dead soldiers, not the sign. Some people have their photo settings set to "public," as did Stone. A few weeks later, someone saw the picture and shared it, which sparked a Facebook page called "Fire Lindsey Stone." After this story went public, local news outlets were showing up at her house trying to get a statement and interview her. As the social media and traditional media scrum continued to grow, she was let go from her job at a center for developmentally disabled adults.

Stop. Think. Do.

Never more true were the words of Warren Buffett, "It takes twenty years to build a reputation and five minutes to ruin it. If you think about that, you'll do things differently."

Let's take an honest look at where a majority of reputation attacks stem from and think about some of the high profile stories that we've heard about.

Do former President Bill Clinton and Monica Lewinsky come to mind? How about Lance Armstrong, who was stripped of all seven of his consecutive Tour de France titles because of illegal use of performance enhancing drugs and bullying his teammates? Not to mention the negative corporate and individual fallout that was felt by his Livestrong Foundation. What about comedian Bill Cosby, who has been publicly accused by, at the time of this book being written, more than thirty women for allegedly drugging and sexually assaulting them? What has happened to his reputation of being a wholesome, family-oriented comedian and role model?

And we haven't seen the full and final impact on people like Harvey Weinstein, Kevin Spacey, Matt Lauer, Bill O'Reilly, and Al Franken, who have all been accused of varying levels of sexual assault or harassment. We do know that legacies and lives have forever been tarnished.

More often than not reputation damage happens because of self-inflicted actions. It stems from internal decisions or lapses in judgment and manifests itself externally when our actions are called into question and publicly scrutinized. The genesis of this book truly was my twenty-plus years of experience in various forms of crisis management where I would look back after a situation was resolved only to find that the person or company I was working with had pulled the proverbial gun out of their own holster, pointed it down at their foot, and squeezed the trigger themselves, seemingly without regard for the impact.

As I asked in the last chapter about the instant replay, how would the lives, reputations, and ultimately the legacies of these people been different had they stopped and thought about the impact of their actions?

Empowered to Shift

The chapters of this book and the personal stories I shared were designed to specifically change your perspective as it relates to your personal reputation, which is truly a living, powerful, and evolving resource.

Early chapters focused first on raising your awareness of the value and impact of your reputation for your personal brand. The landscape in which we live, work, grow, and prosper has forever changed because of technology and social media channels. As the chapters progressed, the storyline shifted to outline strategies that illustrated how you could authentically and proactively enhance your reputation and use it for personal and professional growth, specifically the ideas of the Bank of You, the Reputation Equation, and your Reputation Spotters.

We also covered the power of our reputations and how, when harnessed and intentionally developed, they can lead to greater prosperity and growth through referrals and promotions as well as positive social reviews and feedback.

This final chapter recognizes our humanity. We all make mistakes that impact our reputation. Sometimes that's by saying or doing something without truly thinking through the consequences. Maybe we behave in a way that creates immediate gains, but if discovered could ruin years of hard work? Again, keep in mind that crisis situations are never a question of "if," rather a matter of "when." That is why this chapter will shine a spotlight on the fact that we can (and will) fall, but with consistent work and a focused plan, we will rise again, stronger than ever and be better equipped to move forward to greater personal and professional heights.

It's been said that we are a society that thrives on instant gratification. When we want something, we want it now, regardless of the trade-off—and there are always trade-offs. Maybe you want a new sixty-inch flat-screen TV and you are willing to go into short-term financial debt to get it. However, there are some things in life that just take time and hard work, such as going from account management to the C-suite. Some people find or see ways to short-cut these efforts through less than ethical ways that will deliver instant career gratification while also, unintentionally, going into long-term reputation debt. Remember the one degree of behavior?

In order for a second chance to be truly embraced by others, you must be authentic in your intent, take responsibility for the situation, and be committed to action.

I have planned for, witnessed, and managed dozens of crisis management situations throughout my professional career, and I've become a "student" of reputation management along the way. I purposely use the word student because I am always looking to learn more about this topic, whether that be from within the motorsports industry or in other industries where reputations are made, damaged, and, more importantly, restored.

Through my experiences, I have found that there are four key steps for when a person finds themselves in the Reputation Marbles—whether you are feeling out of control or are up against the wall and think you are out of the race. The reality is that you are never out of the race!

Four Steps for Repairing a Damaged Reputation:

1. Acknowledgment and Ownership:

In October of 1945, President Harry S. Truman had a sign made for him that he placed on his desk at his White House office. The desktop sign read, "The Buck Stops Here." It was a simple message that carried a significant meaning, and one that seems to be lost in our society today. The message was one of personal accountability, ownership of actions and decisions, and the acknowledgment that we are responsible for what we do and the outcome.

How many times have we heard politicians, business leaders, athletes, celebrities, maybe even your friends, colleagues, family members, or boss pass the buck? In other words, people blame someone or something else for what happened rather than take accountability themselves. It never, ever seems to be their fault. Does that make the situation better? Do you respect them more or less for not taking personal responsibility?

The odds are that you lose respect and admiration, not to mention trust, in an individual when they try to rationalize their actions or place the blame anywhere else but where it truly belongs.

Robert Downey Jr. is an amazingly talented and very successful actor. Forbes listed Downey as one of Hollywood's highest-paid actors, reporting that he'd earned an estimated $75 million between June 2012 and June 2013. The Iron Man franchise, which began in 2008 and has been followed by two sequels, has collected more than $2.3 billion globally in sales. And while the money he has made, admiration from his peers and fans he's garnered, as well as awards he's received over the past few years is nothing short of a phenomenal journey, it's probably not the journey for which Downey has the most personal pride.

You may be familiar with Downey's story. He grew up in a Hollywood family and began his acting career in the 1970s. Downey was tapped for roles in a string of hit movies from the mid-'80s through the early '90s that took his talents to main-stream audiences and made him a household name. During an eight-year period, he was busy filming and promoting a string of movie hits, such as *Weird Science, Pretty in Pink, The Pick-Up Artist, Less Than Zero, Air America, Chances Are, Soapdish,* and *Charlie Chaplin,* for which he was nominated for an Academy Award.

It was in the mid-'90s when Downey's drug problems began to surface in a rash of arrests and on-again, off-again rehab stints. Sadly, he said that he was introduced to drugs at an early age by his father. He said to one judge about his relapse that, "It's like I've got a shotgun in my mouth with my finger on the trigger, and I like the taste of the gun metal."

When he finally mustered the strength to own his actions and fully be accountable for the outcomes, it fueled his ability to take ownership of his future. His thoughts on his addiction and journey ranged from humorous, when he said, "I'm allergic to alcohol and narcotics—I break out in handcuffs," to empowered, when he told Oprah Winfrey in a 2004 interview, "It's not that difficult to overcome these seemingly ghastly problems . . . what's hard is to decide to do it."

Downey immersed himself in rehabbing not just his body and mind from addictions but also his reputation, through a steadfast commitment to his craft, regrounding himself in his values, and accountability to his family and colleagues. Over time, he regained the trust of those around him (a movie producer once held back 40 percent of Downey's pay until after shooting concluded to ensure that his addictions wouldn't interfere with production). His work continued beyond the big screen when, in 2010, he became the first and official voice of the iconic Mr. Peanut character for Planters as well as being named the voice-over announcer for Nissan's "Innovation for All" television commercial campaign.

Downey's journey back from the marbles in his life is an extreme one, but I share it for several reasons. The first reason is that while time is of the essence when rehabbing your reputation, it will take just that—time. The second is to illustrate that there has to be commitment to long-term change, which is accomplished by taking ownership of your personal situation and making the right choices each day. Finally, Downey's road to recovery not only led to his reputation being redeemed but also his career. This serves as another example of how it's possible to get caught up in the marbles and by being accountable, recalibrating your values, and diligently living them out, you can lead yourself back to success.

2. Apologize Quickly and Correctly:

It is crucial that once you acknowledge and own a situation, that you then apologize to the individual or group that has been impacted by your actions. Both speed and a proper apology are necessary if this step is to be successful. Why is that?

Let's start with the speed at which you apologize to the person or audience. But, let's first shift perspectives for a moment and think about this from the other side of the table. If someone does something to upset or anger you and they immediately apologize, how does that make you feel? Usually, it will make you feel better, right? Their apology shows that there was not just a quick understanding of how their actions hurt you, but that they want to make you feel better and make the situation right. In a way, the apology validates your initial feelings, but more importantly, you appreciate that the other person quickly recognized it, even if it wasn't their intent to upset you.

Now, how do you feel in that same scenario if the person doesn't apologize to you for a few weeks? More than likely, you will still accept the apology, but your feelings are not quite the same as in the first scenario, right? What's different this time? The longer it takes for an apology to take place, the more questions will pop into our minds when it finally happens. Perhaps you wonder if the person really cares about you or what they did? Maybe you ask yourself if the person had any clue as to what they did and if they even know the impact it had? Does this person only think of themselves? These questions lead to another string of speculation that begins to put pressure on reputations. Why did it take so long to apologize? Are they hiding something? Did someone tell them that they need to apologize instead of them acknowledging themselves, that they should do this? Do they really mean it?

Here's another question for you. Do you know how to make a proper apology? The, "I'm sorry I got you upset" line certainly is an apology, but it's just the first part of a proper one. There are actually three parts to a proper apology.

This is a simple illustration of how the parts come together.

The first part is simply saying that you are sorry for how you made the person feel. "Mary, I'm sorry I angered you."

The second part is to specifically acknowledge what you did to cause anger and briefly describe why or how this happened from your perspective. The key is not to rationalize, defend, or justify your behavior. If you do that, this is no longer an apology, and the focus of the conversation shifts, often to an explanation that can then lead to a debate over the situation. "I know that the way I spoke to you in the meeting came across as being insulting and condescending. That was honestly not my intent. I was just very frustrated with how the meeting was going."

The third part is a critical piece that is often left out of an apology. This part focuses on your commitment to not repeat the action in the future. "Mary, you have my commitment that I will do my best to better channel my frustration in future situations and not have it come out or across at you."

How often do you see someone in your life, maybe a friend or colleague, who acts in a way that upsets or angers you or other friends or coworkers, apologize for it and then do the same thing again the next day or the next week? If this happens on a regular basis, the apologies become hollow and empty and your belief that the person honestly is sorry completely erodes and distrust of that individual will develop.

When you put the three parts together, the apology looks like this, "Mary, I'm sorry I angered you. I know that the way I spoke to you in the meeting came across as being insulting and condescending. That was honestly not my intent. I was just very frustrated with how the meeting was going. Mary, you have my commitment that I will do my best to better channel my frustration in future situations and not have it come out or across at you."

3. Develop Your Plan:

Once you are ready to move forward, it is time to put a reputation recovery plan in place. This will serve as your road map because repairing your reputation takes time and needs to be viewed as a long-term activity if it is to work effectively.

One of the first steps is to genuinely reflect on whatever decisions or actions have led to this situation and see if they align with your values. As I wrote in an earlier chapter, if you aren't grounded in your values, then you must invest time to truly own them and start using them as the basis of your decision-making process. Remember the Reputation Equation as a simple way to place your values as the root of your decisions (Values + Decisions + Behavior + Time = Reputation). The key for the equation to work is that it is based on consistent decisions and behaviors over time. People need to see that you are truly invested in making this change, not just talking about it. This is not a "one and done" fix.

Keith Wyche, a leadership expert and former CEO of ACME Markets grocery chain said in an interview with *Inc.* magazine about reputation rebounds that, "After accepting the consequences, you have to turn inward and take a look at yourself. I call it taking a career selfie. Go back, revisit the situation, and find out what went wrong and what you should have done differently." He goes on to say, "I tell people that I am inspired by my successes but I learn from my failures."

What can you do if your reputation issue is not based on any poor decisions you have made or questionable behavior in which you have participated? What if there was a misunderstanding? Maybe someone took your action the wrong way or heard about what you did second or third hand and what they heard was not what happened? Or, perhaps someone is intentionally trying to attack your reputation and set you back? These are all legitimate situations when it comes to reputation management.

Regardless of whether the reputation crisis stems from a misunderstanding or if it's an intentional smear campaign, it is imperative that you identify the person or persons who are making the claims and directly address the situation. This will allow you the opportunity to accomplish some key points. First, you can discuss the situation and get a clearer perspective of where the misunderstanding developed. Second, if this is intentional, you can assess their motives, even if they don't verbally state them, and, more importantly, let them know you are aware of what they are doing. Third, you can determine if this is a situation that really requires action. For example, if the person who is stirring the pot has a reputation for this, then don't get in the mud with the pig. Do your best to rise above their taunts because sometimes people are just looking for a reaction and the opportunity to throw you off your game. Your intent in these three steps is to resolve the issue quickly and in a mature manner.

The reality is that those last two words, "mature manner," do not always apply to all people. However, by taking this initiative and executing it well—not being accusatory or aggressive—you will already have the high ground and you can control the conversation.

Once you have had these conversations or you have been able to gather enough information as to how or why your reputation is being challenged and you deem that some action is necessary, then it's time to make a few withdrawals from the Bank of You. Identify some of your friends or colleagues that you can talk with about the situation and bring them up to speed on what has transpired. To be clear, this shouldn't be done to hurt or damage someone else's reputation. Remember that you will never look good trying to make someone look bad. The conversation should be factual, regardless of whether it was a misunderstanding or intentional. This is a strategy to tap into your advocates who are in your professional or social circles and can speak for you when you are not there to speak for yourself.

One Sunday morning in March of 2004, I got a call from Crystal Emerick, who was on my public relations team at Nextel. She asked me if I had been on the Jayski website yet that morning. Jayski had become a staple website for all news and rumors related to NASCAR by both fans and those in the industry. I hadn't been on the site that morning, but I could tell by her tone and concern that I was not going to like what I saw there.

As it happened, the night before, one of my senior-level PR managers had taken a few members of the media out to dinner. This isn't an uncommon practice, in fact it's encouraged in order to build relationships (i.e., the Bank of You) or pitch story ideas. Part of the dinner conversation focused on a trend that had been developing at the time, which was having pre-race concerts at the race tracks for the fans—the tracks were doing this as added entertainment value to help offset the high ticket prices. One of the journalists threw out the question to the group at the table as to whether there were too many military elements and tributes in NASCAR pre-race activities. In light of the pre-race concert trend that had been developing, the Nextel PR manager said something to the effect that perhaps fans would want more concerts and entertainment rather than military reenactments. For context, Charlotte Motor Speedway was known for having members of the military reenact the landing and battle in Grenada on the large grass area near the infield start/finish line of the race track. This included soldiers rappelling from helicopters, cannons being lowered onto the "battlefield," and mock buildings being stormed by our soldiers. It was an elaborate show for a fan base that is extremely and passionately patriotic.

The writer essentially took that comment and wrote a small story that appeared in the *Winston-Salem Journal*, "reporting" that Nextel did not support military themes in NASCAR pre-race shows. As you may imagine, this spread like wildfire, and online media outlets and fan forums were running with this story—and the reaction was not praise and support for Nextel! It took about three weeks for the dust to settle, but this is a great example of how one comment can be made, be misunderstood, and inadvertently cause significant reputation issues.

4. Measure Progress:

Reputation recovery is a disciplined practice that requires patience, consistency, and, again, time. Once you have put the previous three steps into play, it is necessary to set up benchmarks for progress. I have outlined several measurement tools by which progress can be gauged, like a Reputation Audit. It can also be reflected in referrals for your business or professional work or just general feedback from colleagues, friends, family, or clients.

Reflecting back on the Nextel story, I spoke with my boss and determined that progress would be measured in three ways—shifting fan sentiment and feedback, reducing the number of media stories on the topic, and getting an apology from the writer and a retraction from the *Winston-Salem Journal*.

The first part was fan sentiment and feedback. The following day, we had gathered up the facts of how this situation came to be and prepared and sent out a statement that was picked up by numerous media outlets and fan forums. Since there was a time lag between people reacting to the initial story and our statement being released, I received more than four hundred e-mails from angry fans accusing us of being everything from anti-American Communists to the living embodiment of the devil himself. I spent the better part of a week responding to each one with a specific message letting them know I read their point of view and included our company statement. My office voice mail was another outlet for ticked-off fans. I recall going into my office that Monday morning after the race and having a full voice mailbox. This particular voice mail system had a capacity for twenty-five messages. Over the next three days, I would empty it in the morning, call each person who left a phone number back, field roughly ten live calls from fans throughout the day and come back to the office the next morning to see that familiar red light on my phone's voice mail indicator and do it all over again. This personal outreach helped shift perspective, change opinions, and not only neutralize fan sentiment but moved it to a positive place for Nextel. I received numerous e-mails stating shock and amazement that someone actually took the time to read their e-mail and respond. Many of the fans posted my response and the company statement to message boards, further helping to quiet and move past the issue.

The second criteria for measuring progress was the number of media stories continuing to perpetuate the false accusation. Day by day there were fewer and fewer online stories being written about this as the motorsports news cycle naturally moved on to the next race. However, to help expedite this, my team did make a few withdrawals from our Bank of You with influential media members who came to our aid once they learned how this story came to be and how irresponsible it had been of the writer to report it.

The third measure was an apology by the writer and a retraction by the *Winston-Salem Journal*. While the damage had been done, getting an apology from the writer was more of a personal acknowledgment that not only what he had written wrong, but that he had made a mistake and understood the harm that was caused by using his news outlet to spread a mistruth. When the newspaper did write a retraction, even though it was buried in the paper, it was another small nod to the fact that they had also made a mistake and gotten it wrong.

Putting it all Together

It takes time, commitment and follow-through to ensure that these four steps come to fruition and allow you to steer through the Reputation Marbles. When I write that it takes time, that actually has two meanings—speed and duration. The speed at which you take ownership and responsibility for what happened as well as make your apology to those involved will demonstrate whether you are authentically owning your actions or merely going through the motions and just doing what you think needs to be done (i.e., "checking the box"). Speed also comes into play with how long it takes you to react to a reputation attack and get your plan into action versus waiting and hoping it just goes away. Duration of time is the other mark of your genuine commitment and how you demonstrate that you will do what you say you will do, with each day's thoughts, decisions, and actions. Your consistency of decisions and actions also support you when someone says or does something to harm your reputation—we should all strive to live in such a way that if someone were to speak poorly of us, no one would believe them.

We all have a limited supply of time and energy as we move through our days and try to get things done. And more often than not, our time and energy is focused on trying to control situations (or sometimes people) to deliver favorable outcomes for us. "There are only so many hours in a day," as the old phrase goes, and we can't control everything. Specifically, we can't manipulate, motivate, or change everyone in our lives. I'm sure you can think of some people who try this on a daily basis. It often is a frustrating and futile endeavor.

And here is a bonus truth—you are not going to make everyone happy all the time. While we know this in our day-to-day analog life, social connectivity has pulled the covers back on the fact that there are trolls out there. Remember my reference to the digital mob mentality? These are people who, generally, hide behind anonymous screen names and love to just pour fuel on social media fires. It's sad, really, but it's a reality. A truth. These are people who are just looking for you, me, and anyone else to trip, stumble, or fall. I write that because I'm not naïve enough to believe that if we do our best each day, that there won't be people lurking, judging, and waiting. I also write that to make a point that we have to rise above those small-minded individuals. Remember, strive to live in such a way that if someone were to speak poorly of you, people would not believe them—our reputations would tell them differently!

TAKE THE WHEEL

Personally, I've come to the conclusion that there are only three things in our lives that we can truly control—our attitudes, our decisions, and our actions. Those three elements are grounded in our values. Who are you? Will you have the right attitude to face and address difficult situations or people? What do you stand for? What do you believe is right? What do you believe is wrong?

Do you have the courage to not only discover these answers, but more importantly, live them out on a daily, consistent basis? That does take courage because it means you are living a life in the minority, as most people find this too difficult, too lofty, or even too aspirational. It doesn't have to be. It can start with just one choice you make today, then again tomorrow and again the next day—that is movement in the right direction. This is why I love the example I shared in an earlier chapter about having a compass for your life and being mindful of how being off by just one degree over the course of a journey can take you to the wrong place. Remember that just one degree can be the difference between recognizing or not recognizing your full potential in the long run.

I was speaking to a leadership class at Davidson College, and at the end of the conversation, one of the students asked me a question that I thought was incredibly insightful. She asked, "Aren't we being fake if we are making decisions to act in a way that would change the way people think of us?" It's a great question that, in my opinion, speaks to the authenticity of our motives and the consistency of our behavior. Think of someone you have known who acts in certain ways around specific people to either get what they want or have others think differently of them. When I think of people like that, and I've known and worked around many over the years, I think of manipulative people whose motive is to change the way they act to look better in someone else's eyes. These are insecure people who have no grasp of their true north.

I asked the student and class the same question. I then went on to share with them, and now you, that this is the challenge before you—how do you consistently live out values-based decisions that lead to authentic behavior?

A fear of mine when writing this book is that I come off "holier than thou." I'm far from it, and I make my share of daily mistakes—I'll own that and always will! However, what I know to be true, from my professional and personal experiences, is that each of us have values that make us unique and exquisite in how we weave them into our lives. My hope for you is that by truly getting your hands around your values, you make decisions and subsequently act in such a way that it is authentically you and no one else. Yes, deliberately and consistently acting in such a way that is aligned with our values can and will impact the way people see us. There is zero manipulation in that, because you are consistently acting in a way and consistently treating people in a manner that is nothing less than you!

There is a simple quote I heard many years ago that has become one of my favorites because it puts the tough experiences we have into perspective. I often use it with my team or when speaking to corporate executives or college students because, in my opinion, it reinforces the fact that we are always learning from life's challenges. Here it goes—"Life is the toughest teacher because you learn the lesson after you take the test."

In essence, we aren't always prepared or equipped to know how to handle situations that come our way in life, and we will make mistakes. More often than not, we learn what not to do after the fact, and if we are truly students of our own lives, we will hopefully be equipped to face and come through similar situations in the future. And as we gain more experience in life, it becomes easier to spot the signs of what is coming at us, which allows us to be more agile and successfully navigate these situations.

The Reputation Economy in which we all live and operate has changed the landscape requiring us to shift the way we value, manage, build, protect, and grow one of our most precious assets. Make no mistake, there will be daily tests and your answers will, over time, define your reputation. But, if you put the elements of this book into play, you will never approach these tests the same, right? Regardless of if you are starting your career, starting a second career, own a small business, an entrepreneur, or in charge of a corporate brand, you now have a game plan to harness, repair, or even leverage the power of your reputation to deliver success and distinction in both your professional and personal life.

In this socially connected and driven world it's easy to feel like your reputation is fair game for anyone who has a voice or can create an online social account. The reality is that reputation issues are never a question of 'if', rather a matter of 'when'! The only real questions to ask are, "Am I prepared?" and "What's my reputation worth?"

SHIFT POINTS:

- We are all human and make mistakes; quickly understand what went wrong and tirelessly demonstrate your amends through action

- There are three parts to a proper apology

- If you fail to plan, you plan to fail; be prepared for a reputation attack/crisis

- Rationalization is not the basis of a plan, nor the way to make decisions

- There will always be people criticizing what you do; rise above them

- Not every personal or business attack is worth fighting. Assess the source, the validity of the issue and subsequent impact—then choose how you should use your energy

- We listen through our own personal filters, which can lead to misunderstandings or unintended reactions; clear communication is vital to success

ACCELERATION:

1. Recall the last time you apologized to someone. Now try reframing the apology in the three-step process on the following lines.

    STEP 1: APOLOGIZE TO THE PERSON

    _____

    _____

    STEP 2: SPECIFICALLY ACKNOWLEDGE YOUR ACTION

    _____

    _____

    STEP 3: COMMITMENT NOT TO REPEAT THE ACTION

    _____

    _____

2. What three actions will you take over the next 14 days to build the foundation of your reputation plan? Will you begin a Reputation Audit? Perhaps you will check your Bank of You balance? Could you refine your "Says Who?" list?

    REPUTATION ACTION 1

    _____

    _____

    REPUTATION ACTION 2

    _____

    _____

Reputation Action 3

3. Circle the statement that you believe is more true for you:

   "I more often rationalize my actions and decisions."

   "I more often own my actions and decisions."

4. List three ways that owning your attitude, decisions, and actions better position you as a leader and fortify your reputation.

   Ownership 1

   Ownership 2

   Ownership 3

Works Cited

Adler, Lou "New Survey Reveals 85% of All Jobs are Filled Via Networking", February 29, 2016, *https://www.linkedin.com/pulse/ new-survey-reveals-85-all-jobs-filled-via-networking-lou-adler*, xix

Allegis Group Services study, August 2012, xix

Chaney, Paul "Word of Mouth Still Most Trusted Resource Says Nielsen; Implications for Social Commerce", April 16, 2012, *https:// digitalintelligencetoday.com/word-of-mouth-still-most-trusted-resource- says-nielsen-implications-for-social-commerce/*, 6

Google/Shopper Sciences U.S., "The Zero Moment of Truth Macro Study", April 2011, *https://www.thinkwithgoogle.com/research-studies/ the-zero-moment-of-truth-macro-study.html*, 9

Chitika, "The Value of Google Result Positioning", June 7, 2013; *https://chitika.com/google-positioning-value*, 26

Brown, Paul "Harnessing the Simple, but Effective Art of Referral Marketing", April 15, 2008, *http://www.nytimes.com/2008/04/15/ business/smallbusiness/15toolkit.html*, 29

Logan, Dave "Why you need to perform a reputation audit today", CBS MoneyWatch, November 17, 2011, *http://www.cbsnews.com/news/why-you-need-to-perform-a-reputation-audit-today*, 42

Jantsch, John "60 Ways to Screw Up the Customer Experience", March 3, 2015, *https://www.ducttapemarketing.com/customer-experience*, 43

Thompson Ph.D., Jeff September 30, 2011, "Is Nonverbal Communication a Numbers Game?", *https://www.psychologytoday.com/blog/beyond-words/201109/is-nonverbal-communication-numbers-game*, 49

Sobal Ph.D, Jeffery & Wansink, Ph.D, Brian, "Mindless Eating: the 200 Daily Food Decisions We Overlook", Cornell University, January 2007, *https://foodpsychology.cornell.edu/research/mindless-eating-200-daily-food-decisions-we-overlook*, 64

Jacques, Amy, "Domino's Delivers During Crisis: the Company's Step-By-Step Response After a Vulgar Video Goes Viral", August 17, 2009, *http://apps.prsa.org/intelligence/TheStrategist/Articles/view/8226/102/Domino_s_delivers_during_crisis_The_company_s_step#.WPpm12nyscU*, 79

eMarketer, "Users Seek Out the Truth in Online Reviews", February 7, 2013, *https://www.emarketer.com/Article/Users-Seek-Truth-Online-Reviews/1009656*, 81

Kasper, Kimberly, "Jobvite Social Recruiting Survey Finds Over 90% of Employers Will Use Social Recruiting in 2012", July, 9, 2012, *http://www.jobvite.com/press-releases/2012/jobvite-social-recruiting-survey-finds-90-employers-will-use-social-recruiting-2012*, 82

CareerBuilder (conducted by Harris Interactive), February 9 – March 2, 2012, *http://www.careerbuilder.com/share/aboutus/pressre-leasesdetail.aspx?id=pr691&sd=4%2F18%2F2012&ed=4%2F18%2F2099*, 82

CareerBuilder (conducted by Harris Interactive), February 9 – March 2, 2012, *http://www.careerbuilder.com/share/aboutus/pressre-leasesdetail.aspx?id=pr691&sd=4%2F18%2F2012&ed=4%2F18%2F2099*, 82

Knowledge@Wharton, "The Hazards of Celebrity Endorsements in the Age of Twitter", February 27, 2013 *http://knowledge.wharton.upenn.edu/article/the-hazards-of-celebrity-endorsements-in-the-age-of-twitter/#*, 96

Rosen, Jeffrey, The New York Times, "The Web Means the End of Forgetting", July 21, 2010, *http://www.nytimes.com/2010/07/25/magazine/25privacy-t2.html?pagewanted=all&_r=0*, 99

Chitika, "The Value of Google Result Positioning", June 7, 2013, *https://chitika.com/google-positioning-value*, 99

U.S. Bankruptcy Court Report, During 12-Month Period Ending December 31, 2014, Table F-2, *http://www.uscourts.gov/sites/default/files/statistics_import_dir/1214_f2.pdf*, 101

Moe, John, NPR Marketplace Tech Report, "The Future of the Internet", September 13, 2010, 102

Nelson, Steve, U.S. News & World Report, "Spitzer Pays More Than $7.5 Million in Prostitution-Related Expenses", *https://www.usnews.com/news/articles/2014/04/28/report-after-prostitute-visits-eliot-spitzer-pays-more-than-75-million*, 103

Radar Staff, "Pay Up, Luv Guv! Eliot Spitzer's Long Suffering Wife Receives $7.5 MILLION in Divorce Settlement – Documents Reveal What Else She Got in the Split From Client 9", April 28, 2014, *http://radaronline.com/exclusives/2014/04/eliot-spitzer-silda-divorce-settlement-luv-guv-ashley-dupre*, 103

Farhi, Paul, Washington Post, "Don Imus Fired by CBS Radio", April 13, 2007, *http://www.washingtonpost.com/wp-dyn/content/article/2007/04/12/AR2007041201007.html*, 115

Pomerantz, Dorothy, Forbes.com, "Robert Downey Jr. Tops Forbes' List of Hollywood's Highest-Paid Actors", July 16, 2013, *https://www.forbes.com/sites/dorothypomerantz/2013/07/16/robert-downey-jr-tops-forbes-list-of-hollywoods-highest-paid-actors/#2f90049b589f*, 119

Yakowicz, Will, Inc.com, "How to Repair Your Damaged Reputation," February 13, 2014, *https://www.inc.com/will-yakowicz/how-to-dust-off-your-reputation-after-falling-in-mud.html*, 124

About the Author

MIKE MOONEY has spent more than two decades in the highly visible sports and motorsports industries creating and executing dynamic communications and marketing programs for global brands, Fortune 500 executives, and athletes. Having worked with some of the most recognizable companies in the world, Mike has successfully launched hundred-million-dollar campaigns, managed dozens of crisis situations, and also reinvigorated brand and personal reputations. The key to his approach for reputation management comes from his first-hand experience and belief that *hope is not a plan*! Success starts with being proactive and identifying potential reputation threats before they become issues. His mindset, and the results he has delivered, has created distinction for his work and respect among the people and brands for which he has worked.

Mike's message and approach has caught the attention of corporate executives and leaders who bring him in to work with their teams to assess reputational threats as well as create plans to spark distinction in their industries. He also has a passion to connect with the next generation of leaders and speaks to college and university student leadership organizations in an effort to drive greater awareness to the power and impact of reputations.

Mike, his wife, and three children live in Charlotte, NC.